THE BABE

A JOURNEY TOWARD SPIRITUAL MATURITY
AND ENLIGHTENMENT

Tina M. Hawkins

ISBN 978-1-68526-834-3 (Paperback)
ISBN 978-1-68526-835-0 (Digital)

Covenant Books
11661 Hwy 707
Murrells Inlet, SC 29576
www.covenantbooks.com

CONTENTS

ACKNOWLEDGMENT

I want to acknowledge the forgiveness, unconditional love, healing, daily provisions, and redemptive guidance of God the Father, the Lord Jesus Christ, the Holy Spirit, and the angelic realm for the grace and mercy that is continually being bestowed upon me through the wisdom that brings about the unquenchable desire to give all glory and honor to God the Almighty.

The forty-year journey from spiritual infancy to realizing the Christian walk and the faith that has empowered my calling toward spiritual maturity has not always been blissful. However, through the love and support of my family and friends, church leaders and members, community activist, and Tyndale Theological Seminary, I have realized what it is to live a balanced Christian life, always ready to teach others and always ready to defend the faith as a kingdom representative.

In addition, I want to give special thanks to my father, Clayton Browning Tyler Jr. Although he was not present in my day-to-day life, the time that we did spend with each other was healing. His presence allowed me to grasp an understanding of the majority of my own characteristics. His knowledge and understanding of scripture and spirituality were incomparable. Rest in love, Dad, and to my beautiful mother, Betty Anne Tyler Williams, who is now resting in the bosom of our heavenly Father, also to my stepfather of forty-five years, Paul Lawrence Williams. Inasmuch as my parents did not always quote the scriptures they studied, they walked the walk instead of just talked the talk. Their daily walk and example displayed the implementation process of God's word. I literally saw them turn one loaf of bread into enough to feed a family of eleven and all others in need. Faith, love, forgiveness, tolerance, and endurance was their shining example to all who graced their paths.

I want to also thank my best friend and husband whose expression of unconditional love, trust, and acceptance has supported me through some very horrific trials and tribulations. His love for Spirit ignited our love and has sustained our twin flame union for twenty years.

I want to thank and acknowledge a dear friend, mentor, and prior supervisor, Amy Craig Vangrack, a director with the Child & Family Service agency's teen parent/independent living programs in Washington, DC. Her unwavering commitment to the sick and suffering ignited my passion of service for a community of lost, abandoned, abused, and forgotten souls. Amy taught me what it was to be a servant and a vessel and that, when providing service to God's kingdom through the foster care and respite group homes, one cannot offer love, empathy, and compassion to the abused alone, that it is absolutely imperative for the healing process to offer that same quality of care to the abuser as well. Afterall, the goal is to assist God in healing the generational curses that has plagued families throughout time.

Last but not least, I want to sincerely thank Leon and Barbara Johnson at Tyndale Theological Seminary for their divine appointments to positions that graced me with the Kay Courtney Courage and Devotion Award used with the bachelor of arts program of study: The Bible and theology. Through the structure, diligent study, guidance, and discipline provided by all the professors that I have engaged, it has enhanced my ability to "study and shew thyself approved unto God" (2 Timothy 2:15). For this, I am eternally grateful. And to you both, I say thank you for believing in me and accepting my essay via text message, henceforth, I am now able to honor God's assignment to complete this manuscript with the confidence required to shed the light on *The Babe: A Journey Toward Spiritual Maturity and Enlightenment.*

INTRODUCTION

The Babe is a spiritually inspired testament exploring the personal forty-year journey of a spirit having a human experience through a Christian's walk from the day of surrender through salvation's process of redemption with the hope of attaining spiritual maturity and the ability to realize a divinely guided and balanced Christian walk.

The Babe explores the parallels between the physical and spiritual birth, growth, and development process and how it is astounding with regard to the outcomes of having received or having not received the proper attention and care as an infant growing into adulthood. In one hand, there is an infant that has received all the necessary love and care since conception to become a productive, loving, and caring member of society. On the other hand, there is an infant that was literally abandoned since conception, being molded by way of the mother's thoughts of termination or disdain, being pierced by the spirit of fear in the womb, whereas, it is known that the baby nestled in womb becomes aware of its outside surroundings at fourteen weeks and responds to the mom's emotional and physical state.

The terminology *babe* is commonly used a metaphor to explain the process of being born again spiritually through the gift of forgiveness and salvation, emphasizing the need for guidance within the body of Christ. It is symbolic of a new creation being birthed into this world, just as a mother gives birth to a child physically, Christ gives birth to the Christian babe spiritually with parallels of them both needing guidance and direction in learning to walk and talk, as well as learning to obtain the proper nutrition through digestible physical or spiritual food, which both should be dependent upon their stages of development. A healthy diet is required for the development of the physical brain and body, just as a proper spiritual diet of God's divinely inspired Word will assure healthy growth and maturity in their daily walk in this world.

Working with the abandoned and abused children of my community and through employment has shown the results of what happens when there is no love, forgiveness, affection, empathy, compassion, knowledge, discipline, structure, or proper diet. The spirit of fear takes root and becomes crystallized in their hearts and minds, which then gives way to the spirit of distrust. So how then are they able to trust the outside world's invitation to salvation? Asking a devastated soul to now trust an unseen God for compassion and love will undoubtedly cause confusion because they were never able to depend on or trust those that they did see every day.

Inasmuch as the physical babe is left without care and guidance, oftentimes the Christian babe is left to fend for themselves without the care and guidance required to understand God's Word and the spiritual realm in which they have now been exposed, becoming easy prey for the onslaughts of negativity, misinformation, and spiritual stagnation, hindering their ability to realize the love, joy, and peace that surpass all understanding through the resurrecting and redemptive qualities of the Holy Spirit's grace, mercy, love, protection, and daily provisions.

My knowledge and experience have shown me that a distorted worldview will create a distorted spiritual view. And as the body of Christ, it is our responsibility to protect and nurture the kingdom baby's spiritual growth and development, just as man's law requires us to adhere to the physical baby's growth and development. It is incomprehensible that we fear man's laws and wrath regarding the babies and that there are those in the family of Christ that totally disregard God's laws and wrath regarding the kingdom babies that He personally chose and called forward to repentance and salvation.

The only difference in the physical and spiritual babe is that the human baby is judged by age, whereas a spiritual baby's age is of no significance because it is determined by the day of surrender. A spiritual baby can be sixty years old at the time of deliverance. Nonetheless, they still have the same beginning as a twelve-year-old.

It is imperative that we cherish our kingdom baby's journey toward maturity and provide them the adequate love, guidance, and protection necessary to become productive members of God's society. Unfortunately, there are those who talk the talk but have no idea how to walk the walk. Judgmental and "fake it until you make it" mindsets have attempted to stagnate God's plan in this world, leaving many suffering in silence and perishing from a lack of knowledge. We must learn and teach by example first. It is so much easier to just have the mind and heart of "do as I say" not "do as I do." However, there are those in the body of Christ that have not faltered in their walk or example, diligently honoring the second coming experience that God has graced them, standing tall and strong as maturing representatives of God the Father, the Lord Jesus Christ, and the Holy Spirit's Christ consciousness.

The point of me sharing what was once too shameful, humiliating, and tragic to utter is because I now believe that complete transparency is imperative before the kingdom and the kingdom babies alike. One's experience, strength, and hope could be another suffering soul's guiding light through the Holy Spirit's process of redemption. It is also a display of God's forgiveness, unconditional love, grace, and mercy toward a suffering and sinful soul.

In no way am I negating God's timing nor His redemptive process, however, I have often wondered, would it have taken all of forty years for me to realize a balanced Christian walk if the pressed-down, resurrected, redeemed, God-fearing Christians in the body of Christ would have embraced me with transparency, unconditional love, forgiveness, guidance, and perspective at the fifteen-year-old onset of deliverance, instead of constant rejection, judgment, gossip, and prying eyes?

Oftentimes Christian babies state that their lives became worse after giving their lives to Christ. No one was there to inform me that receiving the gift of Holy Spirit would begin the rooting process by shedding the light on all deeply embedded sin, whether through self or through the generational curses that have plagued families throughout time. Also, this would be the opportunity for me to release all that had tormented my life. Contrary to some beliefs, most of the horrors in my life came after salvation. It is probably because I was so young when God called me forward. I had not yet begun to live and experience the traps and pitfalls of this world. There was always a sense that it was a good thing that I had given my life when I did because the Holy Spirit covered and protected me through all of the physical and mental abuse, seventeen major surgeries, addiction, molestation, rape, grief, depression, loss, anxiety, abandonment, persecution, and habitual backsliding.

There is an overwhelming amount of information and knowledge provided in Scripture, divinely guided books, lectures, Bible study, and fellowships worldwide that can help halt the perishing process. However, you must be willing to do the work that's required in 2 Timothy 2:15: "To study and shew thyself approved unto God." This means that you will not be able to study, learn, and grow through the efforts of others' sacrifice to understand. You may be able to benefit from their knowledge, but this will not allow you to experience the intimacy of the Holy Spirit and how God will apply His Word to your life and calling daily in the kingdom.

It is my sincere hope that this testament enlightens the hearts and minds of those who feast upon its content. As I stood prepared on and in faith in the streets, group homes, and courthouses of Washington, DC, as a family support specialist/case manager crying out for the abandoned, rejected, exploited and abused babies of our society in the capacity of child protection, I stand now continually being prepared to cry out in fasting and prayer for the health and well-being of the babies of God's kingdom. I stand in complete transparency before the world's judgment in hopes that the body of Christ embrace the kingdom babies with the same love and compassion that Jesus Christ Himself displayed toward all the lives that He encountered. Also, as babes, when we approach scripture, we tend to identify with the character of sin in the testaments. However, as we mature, our goal should to be to identify with God's character throughout the historical accounts. And to remember that, we are under the covenant of the New Testament's grace and mercy. Inasmuch as our society adhere to strict laws and mandates regarding society's babies, I pray that the societies of God's kingdom embrace and nurture the kingdom babies from the womb and bosom of God the Father, the Lord Jesus Christ, and the Holy Spirit with the same gentleness, unconditional love, protection, discipline, guidance, and direction imposed on babies from the wombs of their mothers. Afterall, the kingdom babies will hopefully become the kingdom elders leading the way. So many Christians babies have turned away from God as a result of having to endure the same ravenous atrocities imposed by the evil in the world. What then separates our actions from the world? Maybe if during the onset of deliverance, through devotion, each individual allows God the time to heal their hurt and broken life before they begin the door-to-door mission to save others without truly understanding salvation and redemption themselves through an intimate relationship with their Omnipotent, Omnipresence, and Omniscience Creator. Amen.

IN THE BEGINNING

It was Sunday service in the small-town church that my grandfather resided as pastor decades prior. As I tensely sat with hands and fingers gripping the edge of the aged, hardwood pew, head down, with my feet firmly planted on the warn and faded carpet, the choir's singing began fading into a faint humming. As the pastor opened the doors of the church, tears began to roll down my face as an overwhelming number of thoughts began to flood my mind. It was as though my entire life up to that point had flashed before me just like people have described in near-death experiences. Initially, my thoughts were of the promise made to my girlfriends about joining the church so that I could enjoy the perks of the after-service movie and dinner with friends and local teens alike. It was small-town tradition for the young adults to meet up after service at the local movie theater and then dinner. No service, no movie, or no other weekly freedoms outside of the home. Although a movie with friends was enticing, it had nothing to do with the magnetic force that had begun to pull me from my seat toward the altar. Although the feeling was different, it also felt very familiar and safe. The fear of onlookers' stares and whispers was drowned out by the desire to say that I was sorry. I have no recollection of standing to my feet and moving toward the altar. I remember thinking, *I guess this is what levitation feels like.* It was as though I had experienced a momentary loss of consciousness. When I regained the ability to hear, feel, and stand on my own, I was down on bended knee with my hands stretched toward the sky. As my senses returned, I began to comprehend my immediate environment. I realized that my entire body was engulfed in chills. The pastor and I both were trembling. Following the pastor's instructions, I began to confess with my mouth that Jesus is Lord and that I believed in my heart that God raised Him from the dead, concluding with, "For it is with your heart that you believe and are justified, and it is with your mouth that you confess and are saved."

THE CONTEMPLATION

Inasmuch as I felt an immediate change and shift, I had no idea what the change entailed. Just as I am sure that when a mother gives birth to a baby, that baby is aware of their change in environment, however, just not sure of what that change truly means.

No one explained how serious deliverance and salvation was to daily life, growth, and development, nor did anyone explain the spiritual benefits of giving my life to Christ or that I would now be on Satan's radar for an onslaught of spiritual attacks of the mind, body, and soul. It was simply something that small-town living demanded. The fact that no one from my household were witnesses to what I now know to be the most important decision and act of my life gave me the certainty through the realization that this was between God and I. I returned to my family, my lifestyle, my friends, my temptations, my hurt, my confusion, my lust, my fears, my anger, my resentments, my hatred, and to my fractured personality and ego. I sincerely had no idea what giving my life to Christ truly meant. I knew that I could call myself a Christian and that, if I didn't attend church, I would be the talk of the town. I knew that there would be no extracurricular activities without church attendance. So it is fair to say that I was made aware of the consequences of the basic disobedience in the earthly realm. However, I had no idea what that meant spiritually. I recall the mission being to search out and confront the sinful nature in others through shaming them into submission with the targeted goal being to have them join our church. Having an intimate relationship and journey with the holy Trinity never entered the conversation in theory or example. Nonetheless, the elders, teachers, pastors, and all other leaders, in most cases, lived and followed a different creed. The example that was more often than not displayed was to do as I say, not as I do. It was unthinkable that the same church leaders that had imposed restrictions on my life were still partying with the kingdom babies every Friday and Saturday night at the local Elks lodge. It was also very discouraging that the congregation's confided testimonies and personal tragedies were casually discussed around the dinner tables or over the telephone and during neighborly chatter. I was baffled because the same spirit of disrespect, arrogance, deceit, lust, and greed were the conniving personality, and character defects in myself and in others that ran me away from the streets. That same gang mentality now filled the pews in the church, all of whom appeared to be making no effort to repent or change their evil ways. I say evil because when I did the exact same thing, in most cases based on their example, it was called evil and sinful. It was scary because I thought that I had made a mistake in joining my beliefs to these people. I was in search of something different that would bring about happiness. And because I had no idea of what true and lasting happiness was, I naively trusted what I perceived as God's people. What I found was the blind leading the blind. However, there was a deep sense in knowing that it was not my place to judge other people's behavior, saved or otherwise, primarily because I had no idea what God deemed sinful behavior, nor did I like the way being judged and condemned made me feel.

Just as the physical baby is in need of attention immediately after birth, I felt that I too was in need of immediate care, protection, shelter, guidance, and nutrition to survive the spiritual birth that I was now exposed to. I began to immediately perish from a lack of knowledge at the hands of those God entrusted my deliverance process. My introduction to kingdom life and living was distorted from the very start because I didn't understand God's timing nor the redemption process. Although the three new member's meetings that I was required to attend made me aware of my obligation to the church, they in no way explained God, salvation, redemption, or kingdom requirements. I felt as though I would fail in the mission to gather souls and lead them to salvation and church membership because I simply had no idea of who or what this new creature in

Christ entailed; so how then could I spread the good news of salvation. No one told me that Jesus Christ had already secured our salvation with His death at the cross or that there was absolutely nothing that I could do to earn what was freely given.

SALVATION

Romans 10:1–13 explains, "Brothers, my heart's desire and prayer to God for them is that they may be saved. For I bear them witness that they have a zeal for God, but not according to knowledge. For, being ignorant of the righteousness of God, and seeking to establish their own, they did not submit to God's righteousness. For Christ is the end of the law for righteousness to everyone who believes. For Moses writes about righteousness that is based on the law, that the person who does the commandments shall live by them. But the righteousness-based faith says, 'Do not say in your heart, 'Who will ascend into Heaven?' *(that is, to bring Christ down)* or 'Who will descend into the abyss?' *(that is, to bring Christ up from the dead)*. But what does it say? 'The word is near you, in your mouth and your heart' *(that is, the word of faith that we proclaim)*; because, if you confess with your mouth that Jesus is Lord and believe in your heart that God raised Him from the dead, you will be saved. For with the heart, one believes and is justified, and with the mouth one confesses and is saved. For the Scripture says, 'Everyone who believes in Him will not be put to shame.' For there is no distinction between Jew and Greek; for the same Lord is Lord of all, bestowing His riches on all who call to Him. For 'everyone who calls on the name of the Lord will be saved.'"

"[1]Paul's prayer for Israel, who had zeal, without knowledge of, or subjection to, God's righteousness: fundamental contrast between the righteousness of doing and that of believing. Here, Paul addressed all saints concerning his yearning for national salvation. The words my *heart's desire* are literally "the dear pleasure of my heart." Israel's

---

[1]   William R. Newell, *Romans Verse-by-Verse*, chap. 10, page 387–389.

salvation was to Paul a thing of delight to contemplate and hope for. Moreover, as always, Paul put his wish for them into prayer to God in which all spiritual longings should end. But it was certainly a terrible thing we see. Here was the Jew with God's own book of the Old Testament scripture in his hand and blind to that scripture's revelation of his guilty, lost state before God. The Jews were in a fearful condition. They were wholly ignorant of the one great, vital fact sinners must know: that righteousness, life, and all things are a free gift of the grace of God and that the law was not meant only to make them discover their sin and their own helpless need of the outright gift of righteousness from God. The expression *ignorant of God's unrighteousness* does not mean that the Jewish people were ignorant of holiness and righteousness as attributes of God; in fact, they prided themselves on the knowledge of such a God as over against the hideous pagan gods. But the righteousness of which they were wholly ignorant was that while "God Himself was just," He was also, "the Justifier of the ungodly," of all who "believed on Jesus." Christ came, although born under law in order to redeem Israel (Galatians 4:4–5), yet He Himself, from the very beginning, took the place of the law! In the Sermon on the Mount (Matthew 5, 6, and 7), He declared, "It was said, but I say," He came indeed, not destroy but to fulfill, and inasmuch as Israel was under the curse of the law, he redeemed them that were under the law, becoming Himself a curse for them. (Galatians 3:13).

I am truly grateful to God for allowing me the opportunity to journey back to my spiritual beginnings with the wisdom of the now fifty-five year-old's experience and knowledge to hopefully reach that fifteen-year-old's broken heart and misguided understanding of salvation, bringing about true harmony within self today.

I would first say thank you, Tina, for never giving up, regardless of the persecution, psychological and physical torture and abuse, misinformation, and rejection from those that you trusted. Thank you for continually offering service through love and support to those less fortunate. Thank you for always questioning what instinctively made no sense and learning to research and study for self-clarification. Thank you for keeping the focus on our walk instead of others.

Thank you for utilizing the faith of a mustard seed and believing in our intuitive abilities and prophetic dreams. In addition to you being able to follow your heart and set aside your opinion of others in the church and community, you were then able to become a vessel of service to God's hurt and suffering children. With the act of following your heart and intuition, setting aside your unfounded opinions of your new church family's walk with Christ and keeping the focus on your intimate journey with holy Trinity, you were allotted to embrace your first act of moving in faith by letting go and letting God. Inasmuch as you demonstrated faith in believing that the lives of both self and all other believers were surrendered to God's power to heal and change character through His divine timing and process of redemption, you offered another suffering and sinful soul the same unconditional love that God, Jesus Christ, and the Holy Spirit provides you daily through provisional grace and mercy. Although you may not understand now without seeing the big picture, rest assure that it will all make sense soon. The very things that you will be made to feel shame and guilt over will be your future testimony of God's forgiveness, salvation, and redemption. You are the perfect blend of your father's intelligence and ability to research, memorize, and teach others with intention and charisma, and your mother's ability to impactfully implement God's word in daily life. I love you, and there would absolutely be no me without you. Your faith and endurance ignited my life. And throughout all the trials and tribulations that we have overcome through the grace and mercy of God the Father, the Lord Jesus Christ, and the Holy Spirit, you never stop believing, and you never give up.

THE WALK BEGINS

Here I sit, slouched over, head in lap, trying to find a comfortable position in this hard metal folding chair that continues to wobble from side to side. I am really trying to make the best of what I see as a bad situation. Meanwhile, the therapist leading this 8:00 p.m. inpatient mandatory twelve-step meeting of Alcohol and Narcotics Anonymous began randomly selecting folks to share their story because no one would volunteer. I was hoping and praying that she did not call on me. Afterall, I had no advice to give because this was my third time checking into a facility due to my inability to be honest with myself and live life soberly on life's terms.

I was completely baffled at how birthday celebrations, family reunions, cookouts, and happy hour landed me in this state and in this place. I recalled the summer of 1977 as Marvin Gaye's new hit song "Got to Give It Up" blared through window fans from nearly all the houses on my sheet. It was like a block party every day. There is nothing like DC in the summertime. The teenage boys were mimicking Bruce Lee's latest moves; the elderly were sitting cozy on their porches with a glass of iced tea; the young adults were shining their cars as the girls braided their afros; more often than not, the parents were gathered together over a card game of spades or bid whist, while my crew and I competed against each other through cheerleading competitions. Wow! What a time. The cheerful and joyful faces of those that were popping bottles did not display anguish, depression, and suffering. My perception was that drinking alcohol was commonplace during life's celebrations. Their faces did not show the aftereffects of the hangover, poor health, inability to maintain employment, or the broken relationships that followed, nor did it display the awareness that alcohol and drug addiction leads to jails, institutions, and an early grave. As I perished from a lack of addiction knowledge, I honestly thought that there was something seriously wrong with me because I didn't respond the same to alcohol as the functioning alcoholics that surrounded me daily. Although my mother was a young single mother of eight children that would drink occasionally, she would make sure that we were fed, bathed, and safely tucked in bed before she would enjoy drink while listening to the Quiet Storm evening radio broadcast. However, I do recall a time when my mother's friends and family would stop by to entice her to drink with them because things weren't doing so well. It was probably because my mom seemed to always have it together, even though she was the one raising eight children in the midst of her husband and father of her children abandoning her, as well as all of the daily stresses of trying to survive in this world with eight children and her mother without the western world's sense of education. No one knew that drinking in front of a child, with an addictive nature through genetics, would bring about a lifetime of heartache, low self-worth, daily struggles for sobriety, and serious health issues due to obesity.

That's the nature of this disease—cunning, baffling, and very deceptive. It is described as an obsessive, compulsive disorder. As the mind obsesses over the drug or alcohol, it creates an urge to use. Once you have consumed the drug of your choice, it creates the physical compulsion to continue using as well as a losing control. "[2]The American Society of Addiction Medicine defines addiction as a treatable, chronic medical disease involving complex interactions among brain circuits, genetics, the environment, and an individual's life experiences. People with addiction use substances or engage in behaviors that become compulsive and often continue despite harmful consequences. There are substance addictions and nonsubstance addictions, which include gambling, food, Internet, gaming, cell phone, and sex. There are primary indicators of an addictive nature and use."

---

[2]   The American Society of Addiction Medicine, *Addiction Medicine*, copyright 2019, all rights reserved. ASAM.org.

As the therapist continued to select individuals to share, I began to sit upright in my battered chair and attempted to make eye contact with each person sharing, realizing that our stories of heart breaks and disappointments were definitely more alike than different. These meetings left me in amazement. I had never witnessed such transparency and honesty with the oath of anonymity. Every meeting that I attended, mandatory or otherwise, left me in awe. Whether it was day or night, inpatient or outpatient, a group of strangers from every race, age, gender, religious, or atheist sect stood hand in hand, reciting the Lord's Prayer in unison. I witnessed salvation and redemption in action through their powerful stories of experience, strength, and hope. I watched them coddle the newcomer, *the babe*, with supportive resources, unconditional love, and direction with the guidance of the Holy Spirit. They proclaim to be a spiritual program as opposed to a religious one. This was a devastating blow as a Christian to witness atheist, Hindus, Buddhist, Muslims, Jehovah's Witnesses, and Christians alike all recited the Lord's Prayer quoted in Matthew 6:9–13 of the Christian Bible before and after every meeting, and I was yet to hear the Lord's Prayer recited by the prayer warriors of the churches that I had attended up to this point. It is the prayer that our Lord and Savior left for us. It is thorough and all inclusive, replacing the "I" with "we and us." I watched as trust and belief in this prayer transformed the lives of those that society condemned and threw away.

Listening attentively to all the life testaments that were being shared taught me that one should never judge a book by its cover. These people represented all walks of life. There were doctors, teachers, police, successful business owners, athletes, construction workers, clergymen, students, etc. Although these people would get high during good times, bad times, when the sun was shining, when it was rainy, and so forth, these incredible stories of triumph restored my hope in mankind and God again. I also realized that I had been sick in soul long before I had picked up a drink or drug. Addiction was just the outward display of the agony within. Finally, God led me to place that I could feel free to open up about the hurtful atrocities that I had endured and that had stolen my dreams, beauty, health, daily provisions, as well as having stunted my mental and spiritual growth and development.

I guess fleeing small-town Virginia in the middle of the night to return to the streets of Southeast DC was not all that I had hoped for. The one thing that I knew for certain was that returning home to city life, everybody here did not know me or my business, unlike the town that my mom and dad's families were from. She packed us up and left DC to give us a sense of family and village living. The problem for me was that I no longer trusted the village. I truly loved and missed DC and the friends that I grew up with from elementary through junior high school. I felt as though Southeast DC was my garden of Eden. It was the place where I became consciously aware of myself, my family, and the outside world. The place where I became aware of my nudity and began to cover up, where I ate the forbidden fruit that my parent had warned of the dangers and knowledge thereof, where my rebellion against God and earthly authorities began, where I was deceived by the serpent nature in man and self, and where I began to try and cover up and hide away from God in guilt and shame.

When I arrived back in DC, things began to move really quickly. Before I knew it, running had become a thing for me, whether through changing geographical locations or running away mentally and emotionally through sex, drugs, food, gambling, alcohol, shopping etc., you name it. I used whatever distraction that was available! The addictive nature that I was told that I suffered with by way of the family tree had landed me in a psych ward again at age twenty-five. I would surrender to a different facility each time because I was too ashamed to return to the prior one. As usual, the treatment facilities, schools, jobs, churches and all other affiliates had deemed me the most likely to succeed. Meanwhile, the isolation of shame and guilt became crippling. You know what I find interesting? The same isolation that once completely drove me insane is the same isolation that I live for today. I thrive for the calm serenity and peace and quiet that it brings about.

THE FEAR OF UNCERTAINTY

It was discharge day, and I was terrified of myself and my latest choices. Inasmuch as I was ready to leave this place, I was a nervous wreck due to the uncertainty of my willpower to sustain. All that I was leaving with were the clothes on my back and a narcotics and alcohol anonymous pamphlet in one hand, highlighting the first step in recovery; a pamphlet highlighting the serenity; and Lord's Prayer in the other. I was returning to a lifestyle that had no idea of my recent changes. I was trying my best to stay calm because the anxiety that I w0sm experiencing could be mistaken as the anxiety of an urge to get high. It was suggested that I should get a sponsor to guide me through the terrifying rigors of early sobriety. We were able to find these sponsors at the meetings and that it was important to choose someone with at least five years of sobriety. It was assured that the blind could only lead the blind back to drinking and getting high. We were continually reminded that it was easier for us to be pulled back into the bar scene than it would be to pull others out, also that it was not a good idea to go back in search of praise from those that witnessed our demise. It is enticing to want to show others that you have bathed and gained back weight; however, you must be honest with yourself about wanting to go back around the toxic environment that led you to hell on earth. Initially, I thought that the discussions entailed what, when, and how we used. But much to my surprise, they taught relapse prevention and coping skills when attempting to accept life on life's terms. First and foremost, I witnessed the theory of God's salvation, forgiveness, unconditional love, protection, guidance, redemption, grace, and mercy implementation process.

It seemed as though the hour that I had been waiting for my ride to pick me up took forever. It was not by mistake that God was allowing me more time to reflect and contemplate my next moves, which should have been to go straight to a meeting, especially because I was overwhelmed with fear and anxiety. The scripture in Matthew 6:10 says, "As above, so below" began to reveal to my heart that this scripture, in the literal sense, could also mean that the mind, being above, dictates to the body, which is below. The mind's obsessions and desires create the body's urges for that particular thing. As thoughts flooded my mind, my heart began racing as tension attacked my body in the form of severe muscle spasms. This was it! Do-or-die time! I closed my eyes and started the pragmatic breathing techniques taught in the coping mechanism workshops. As I clutched the pamphlets in hand, I began reciting the Lord's prayer as practiced daily in treatment.

"[3]Our Father, who art in heaven, hallowed be thy name, your kingdom come, your will be done on earth as it is in heaven. Give us this day our daily bread. And forgive us our debts, as we forgive our debtors. And lead us not into temptation, but deliver us from evil. For thine is the kingdom, the power, and the glory" (Matthew 6:9–13). Amen.

This prayer is an affirmation of truth—truth about ourselves, our relationships, the daily temptations and struggles of this world, our relationship to God, and our power and potential through prayer in the physical world.

I am so grateful that our Lord and Savior took the time to deliver this prayer for us in the midst of all the he was experiencing during that time. Thank you, Jesus!

Afterward, I began reciting the Serenity Prayer: "[4]God, grant me the serenity to accept the things that I cannot change, the courage to change the things that I can, and the wisdom to know the difference."

The understanding that I have of this prayer is to let go of situations beyond our control and to take action toward the things that are within our control.

---

[3]   *The MacArthur Study Bible*, "The Lord's Prayer," Matthew 6:9–13.
[4]   Reinhold Niebuhr, The Serenity Prayer, 1892–1971.

As I continued to cry out to God for His grace and mercy in facing the day and all that entailed, I began reciting the first step of Alcohol and Narcotics Anonymous. "[5]We admitted that we were powerless over our addiction and that our lives have become unmanageable."

This proclamation of daily surrender meant that I was admitting to myself and others before God that I had acknowledged a problem that no human power could resolve, also that I have not been able to control it with my own willpower; and as a result, it creates self-destruction in my life and the lives of others that I encounter. It is very important because denial is the primary component in fueling addiction of any kind. How can you be healed from something that you don't know exists? Once you admit that you have a problem, then one can begin to seek healing assistance. Alcohol and Narcotics Anonymous representatives believe that it is necessary to admit that you cannot control your addiction, and as a result, you cannot manage your day-to-day life any longer. It is also suggested that you play your life's tape from beginning to end before choosing relapse. This means that I had to honestly go back through the horrors that I had experienced or witnessed and the outcomes in their entirety. Addiction has a way of seducing the mind and heart into believing that you were having the time of your life. It also seems to exclude the pain and suffering endured. More than not, we tend to stop the tape at the good parts because no one wants to relive the humiliating pains and hardships of losing their family, employment, home, pride, dignity, freedom, physical appearance, trustworthiness, and deceptive ways. I had used to block out my tape. To relive the horrors of people being skinned alive or being fed their own feces as a result of a fifty-dollar debt to the drug dealers did not scream sobriety, nor did I want to remember how alcohol addiction caused my grandmother's head to swell three times its size as a result of liver and kidney failure or the terrifying night I was told that my younger brother stabbed my older brother to death while high. This was not

---

[5] Bill W., *The Big Book*, Alcohol/Narcotics Anonymous, published April 10, 1939. OCLC: 408888189.

something that I wanted to replay in my mind or heart. It was bad enough watching the streets of our nation's capital turn into a scene from the movie *The Night of the Living Dead*. Enslaved family members, friends, and neighbors roamed the streets in a vicious cycle of using, buying, and doing whatever to get more at three in the morning. I have often wondered why destroying something is so much easier than putting it back together.

TEMPTATION OR TEST

I checked into a motel on the outskirts of DC. I told myself that I wanted to get as far away from the streets of Southeast as possible. A hot shower and a light meal were just what I thought that I needed. However, I ended up sitting alone with my thoughts staring at the walls and trying to wrap my head around where my choices had landed me. All of my best thinking had landed me in treatment—depressed, angry, frustrated, and overwhelmed with guilt and shame. Inasmuch as my thinking led me to a place of solitude, it also set me up for failure. When my thinking suggested alone time over a meeting upon release as was suggested, I realized that I had taken back my will from God and those that He placed in my path for healing. The more that I attempted to play the tape of how I reached this point, the more that I wanted to disappear into a fifth of Remy Martin VSOP.

Of course I called a girlfriend that I used with instead of one of the sober women that I had met during the impatient meetings. The bad part about relapsing right out of treatment is that getting high or drunk will not drown out all of the reprogramming that you received over a consecutive twenty-eight-day period. The spiritual based sobriety quotes and the faces of those who shared their daily testaments of sober living consumed my heart and mind. What I also realized was that I had already relapsed in my mind and heart before actually using. I continued to hear the AA/NA quote: "One drink is too many, and a thousand is never enough." I truly did not know if this was a test or temptation. What I did know was that I had failed. After being seduced by the spirit of addiction, I was left feeling like a failure, and the spirit of depression ensued. The question that I had to ask myself was whether or not I would stay down after tripping and falling, or would I get up and do what had been proven to work? It was then that I was reminded that for some people, relapse was a part of their recovery. Hopefully, I would see the mistakes that I made and be willing to do what was necessary to allow God's guidance and gentle hand to fix them. The scariest part of addiction and recovery is that you may not make it back. I have witnessed countless people that have died by way of overdose right out of treatment, institutions, and jails. Attempting to realize step one was a hard pill to swallow because I had to admit complete defeat and powerlessness. In addition to having an allergy to all mood- and mind-altering substances, I also had an allergy to the party scene, people, places, and things that were celebratory. Even if I changed frequency, types to get high, or places to get blasted, they would all lead me to the same places that many suffering addicts end up.

The obsessive-compulsive mind and personality disorder that had plagued so many families had no boundaries or borders based on race, age, gender, education, or religion. The disease of addiction may rear its cunning and baffling head, disguised as food, sex, gambling, etc. It also leaves a path of tormented, abused, and heartbroken families and friends. In addition to the destruction of the neighborhood and community as a whole, it leaves people living under the cloak of the constant fear of being robbed or attacked, devaluing the property that many have sacrificed and worked by the sweat of their brow to receive and maintain. Unlike most cities, DC is not separated by gangs or colors; DC is ran by neighborhoods. The dangerous part is that you have no idea who's the enemy. You wander into the wrong community, and there will definitely be a young child or a grandparent in the midst of the mob attacking you. A lot of the rapes and robberies happened as a result of desperation, leading addicts to dangerous places to buy drugs from dangerous people under the cloak of darkness.

Contemplating whether my relapse was a result of me failing at temptation or test consumed my thinking. I truly did not believe that God would tempt me this early in recovery. However, I did believe that this was a test and opportunity to implement the biblical and Alcoholics and Narcotics Anonymous based theories that I had studied during treatment. Temptation creates the pressure to give into one's ungodly desires—desires that influence us to turn away from God. I don't believe that temptation is a sin; it is giving into the temptation that causes us to sin.

> [6]Blessed is the one who endures trials, because when he has stood the test he will receive the crown of life that God has promised to those who love Him. No one undergoing a trial should say, "I am being tempted by God," since God is not tempted by evil, and He Himself doesn't tempt anyone. (James 1:12–13)

> [7]No, in all these things we are more than conquerors through Him who loved us. (Romans 8:37)

> [8]You are from God, little children, and you have conquered them, because the one who is in you is greater than the one who is in the world. (1 John 4:4)

The late teens and early twenties are a time of great challenge and uncertainty. Emerging adults have left adolescence but are some distance from taking on adult responsibilities. "[9]Emotional and social development in early adulthood is explained as emerging adulthood, which greatly prolongs identity development, released from the oversight of parents but not yet immersed in adult roles. Ages 18–25 years old can engage in activities of the wildest possible scope because so little is normal or socially expected. Routes to adulthood responsibilities are highly diverse in timing and order across individuals.

---

[6] *The MacArthur Study Bible*, "Temptation," James 1:12–13.

[7] *The MacArthur Study Bible*, "Conquerors," Romans 8:37.

[8] *The MacArthur Study Bible*, "He Who Is Greater," 1 John 4:4.

[9] Galambos, Barker, and Krahn, *Early Adulthood*, 2006, Montgomery/Cote, 2003.

Furthermore, exposure to multiple viewpoints encourages development of a more complex self-concept that includes awareness of their own changing traits and values over time, along with enhanced self-esteem."

The confusion of having your parents', educators', and employer's programming regarding mastering the ability to create your own path, dreams, and future is conflicting with the biblical perspective of God's will being done in God's own timing, as well as learning to live in the grace of the here and now. When these lessons were being taught, no one left the room for the possibility of those who would be in need of constant guidance and structure to survive the path laid before them.

The treatment counselors had also recommended that I get involved with a church and community service. The difference between the small-town church that I had given my life to Christ in and the many churches of Washington, DC was that there were so many to choose from. I had no idea the Christian church was so divided by denominations. In addition to all the other ritual-based churches, our nation's capital was a melting pot for different cultures and religious beliefs. I had experienced so much since giving my life. I truly thought that maybe they did not do something right. After all, there was absolutely no way that I could change myself to please God at this point. My lack of faith and understanding led me to repeat the process of surrender and baptism at a local church. No one explained repentance to me, so I thought that each time that I fell short, a new ceremony would be required to move forward.

I was blown away when psychologist explained that the age in which you begin consuming drugs, alcohol, and/or cigarettes would be the age that your brain development would be stagnated. This meant that when I began drinking and smoking at age fifteen, I literally began to stunt my brain development and mental capacity. Henceforth, I am still a fifteen-year-old in a twenty-five-year-old's body and lifestyle, unable to comprehend and respond as a maturing adult. Although the people around you believe that you are an adult physically based on age, most have no idea that they are dealing with temper tantrums and whimsical behaviors of an angry, confused, immature teenager that may not understand the task of the adult society that they find themselves living and working amongst. I had to begin my sober journey by first addressing the issues of that fifteen-year-old and with the daily guidance and direction of the Holy Spirit I would begin learning to live an age-appropriate lifestyle.

THE WILDERNESS

Historically God has used the wilderness to speak with His people. Just as God spoke to Abraham in the wilderness, He also led the Israelites into the wilderness to speak to them at Mount Sanai. Symbolically, the wilderness is signified as a place that is uninhabited and uncultivated in a spiritual sense, a place where the truth had not been joined with good yet, a place of intense experiences that requires nourishment to survive, a place of dangers and divine deliverance, of isolation, of renewals and divine encounters with God, such as the burning bush experience.

I thought that the wilderness was a place to run rampart under the guise of being a productive member of society. I absolutely loved the freedom of running wild in hopes that no one that knew my mother would see or witness my wicked and disgraceful behaviors. However, I now understand it to be a place of learning and evolution, a place where my testimony was forged.

THE BONDAGE OF SIN

Sin was explained to me as an immoral act. According to Augustine of Hippo 354–430, "Sin is a word, deed, or desire in opposition to the eternal law of God." Scripture states that sin is the transgression of the law. Inasmuch as the New Testament defines sin as a personal offense against God, sin cannot do anything to God.

"[10]The four types of sin are sins of commission, sins of omission, venial sin, and mortal sin. The sin of commission are those sinful actions that are proactively done, such as, lying, idolatry, swearing, and murder. The sins of omission occurs when you fail to obey God's moral laws, such as a person that fails to do something which they are able to do and which they ought to do but have put themselves in a situation whereby they are unable to complete the task. For example, a person that gets drunk, knowing they had a task to perform and are now unable to execute it physically because they knowingly put themselves in that position. Venial sins are less serious than mortal sins because they do not destroy our relationship with God and our ability to love. Mortal sins are a more serious offense against God. It is explained as a gravely sinful act, which can lead to damnation when its quality is such that it leads to separation of that person from God's saving grace."

I had no idea that there were various levels of sin or that there were conscious sins that I am aware of and unconscious sins that I may not be aware of. I recall the seven deadly sins as being vanity/pride, sloth, gluttony, lust, avarice, envy/jealousy, and wrath/anger; however, I only understood the surface level of those sins. I consider vanity/pride to be a form of self-idolatry in which a person attaches

---

[10] Katelyn Kleisinger, "The 4 Types of Sin," Prezi Inc. 2022, Prezi.com.

themselves to the greatness of God for the sake of their own self-praise and image. Sloth is a sin against God in which one refuses the joy and divine goodness, losing the hope in ever achieving what God desires of them to accomplish, leading to eternal happiness. Gluttony is described as excessively overindulging, which also covers greed. In addition to lust being attributed to rape, adultery, wet dreams, seduction, unnatural vices, and fornication, it can also be to salivate over something or someone that God had not ordained for you to have, such as the avarice in excessive desires for wealth or gain. Envy and jealousy are when one covets or desires to have what someone else has. Anger is described as strong feelings of hostility, which undoubtedly brings about the wrath of divine chastisement.

Wow! My addictive nature and lifestyle over the past ten years has exemplified the definitions of sin, and yet God still covers me with His forgiveness, unconditional love, protection, and daily provisions in spite of me and where my journey has led me up to this pivotal point in my life. A major problem in my thinking is that I have been looking for and judging myself and others for what only God the Father, the Lord Jesus Christ, and Holy Spirit can provide. Please forgive me! I am a divine work in its process.

❇

WHO AM I NOW

The programming as well as the religious and cultural biases in this world have made us all feel less than. Everybody wants to be someone else or somewhere else. We take issues with our gender, race, age, physical appearance, economic standing, and so forth. We have been programmed to only see the sinful lawbreakers in each other instead of seeing one another as God's children. We are so quick to covet, judge, and condemn each other rather than see ourselves as a work of God's art as clay being shaped and molded in His image. I feel as though, if God could love and forgive each of us, then we should at least be able to show a little empathy as well.

"[11]Romans 12:21 says, 'Do not be overcome by evil, but overcome evil with good.'" This verse follows exhortations, such as, 'Bless those who persecute you' (verse 14), and 'Do not repay anyone evil foe evil' (verse 17). The theme of this passage is how to love with sincerity (verse 9), requiring us to set aside our judgments. God is challenging our flesh to live at higher levels by the Holy Spirit's power. Of course, the human way is overcome evil with evil. According to Romans 12:21, we can only overcome evil with good because His goodness is stronger than any evil. Just as Jesus did when they insulted, tortured, and nailed Him to a cross, Jesus Himself fully surrendered to the will and plan of His Father. The Son of God showed by example and overcame evil with good. Although the actions against Jesus was evil, Jesus's death and resurrection overcame that evil by purchasing forgiveness and eternal life for everyone who believes. It is absolutely imperative to get to know the character of God and how He truly loves His creations. Unlike man's love and care, God's love

---

[11] *The MacArthur Study Bible*, "Do Not Be Overcome by Evil," Romans 12:21.

is truly divine and unconditional. The problem is that most human beings have no idea of what love is or represents. Our perception of physical love has distorted our perception of spiritual love. The same mouth that is used to say that they love you is the same mouth used to curse, shame, and condemn. The same heart and mind used to offer love and kindness is also used to manipulate and abandon you. The same hands used to offer the comfort of love is the same hands used to beat, lock up, starve, evict, shoot, and throw away God's children as they sign the divorce papers. The image of self starts in the womb and the continual programming from that point. Early on, your self-image is linked to your parents. If your parent's display is that of shame and disgrace, henceforth, your identity will begin to mirror that behavior because it is what you witness every day and are encouraged to follow. As one journeys out into the world, they begin to see and experience different mindsets and lifestyles. However, it is absolutely taboo to bring that newfound reality back home with you because this would undoubtedly create an adverse environment. It is easier to follow suit than it is to break generations of a particular belief, behavior, or mindset, especially when you are reliant upon them for your basic daily survival. Conflicting dynamics of basic human nature has wreaked havoc on our communities as a whole. The basic arguments of 'nature versus nurture' is often presented as the model. Various religious beliefs, parenting skills, academics, economic challenges, and what is viewed in our media has dictated the new norms. When I was a young girl, I aspired to be a wife, mother, teacher, doctor, writer, or business owner, as did all the other girls that I knew. Today the normal aspirations for so many young girls are to be a stripper, side chick, or a video vixen. It is so unfortunate that women fought for the rights of self-identification and pride, and now the idea of high self-worth and esteem has been shunned and devalued, resulting in one's self-worth revolving around the number of followers that one has after exposing their personal lives and/or body through pornographic gestures, acts, or exposing the appearance of their decaying flesh. Red-bottom, high-heeled shoes should not determine where a person has been or are going in life. There are so many titles and psychological programs that contradict who and what God says that we are as believers. The fact is that most believers are still identifying with the likeness and character of their earthly father's title, example, and character rather than their heavenly Father's title, example, and character.

Surprisingly, as we attempt to prepare our babies for the harsh realities of this world, whether through emotional or spiritual support and guidance or discipline and structure, we can only hope and pray that our moral code of ethics take root in their hearts, minds, efforts, and deeds. The issue with perspective is that everyone does not share the same viewpoints on morals and ethics. We send our seeds into this world as our younger representatives to honor God, the family name, and household. A major concern is that they will encounter individuals who do not share the same realities. I recall having to dumb myself down in appearance and intelligence to make it safely home from school every day. Although my family thought that my sixteen-inch dark curly hair was absolutely adorable, against my red-bone complexion, draped over my tall, slender build, not everyone else in southeast felt that way. Straight As and perfect attendance was highly praised by my family; however, it put a target on my back, resulting in a constant attacks of demeaning verbal and sometimes physical abuse by classmates. I believe that this was when my personality first began to split. I had to be one way at home and another at school. As kids, we are told to take pride in our appearance and to be the best that one could be. But there are hurt and angry individuals in this world that would beat all the beauty off your face and out of your heart, slowly turning a wondrous dream into a horrible nightmare for all involved. You stop raising your hand in class when you know the answer. Your attitude and wardrobe have transformed into unrecognizable, even to one's self. In addition to your family's image of who and what you are to be, there is a public and private school sector's grading scale, which now determines your ability and worth going forward. This factor will create your demographic reality and daily existence. Inasmuch as titles continue to attach themselves to you, your cultural and religious biases will dictate the norm, leaving the heart of the fifteen-year-old original dreamer wondering what happened all together, all the while, living in the midst of those that will never allow you to move forward from your past deeds. The good news is that you are now a member of God's family and kingdom. There is absolutely nothing that you have to prove to anyone at any time. As the Holy Spirit's process of redemption began to peel back the layers of hurt, pain, misinformation, shame, and guilt, the identity crisis will no longer exist in your heart and mind as your persecutors witness God raise you as a phoenix from the ashes of doubt and self-condemnation.

Ages zero to fifteen was the first pivotal point in life. Whereas, I am beginning to understand and comprehend the world around me and utilizing my will in making daily choices without parental influence, age twenty-five was the beginning of the second pivotal point in my life. Whereby I am now beginning to understand the results of my choices and how they impact the world around me physically and spiritually.

The external influences of addiction that subdue our ability to properly reason with ourselves and the outside world creates a diversion from the path most traveled. In addition to stunting one's physical and mental growth and development, it also hinders one's ability to function at an age-appropriate level. The atrocities that follow a lifestyle of addiction further adds to the karmic cycles of backsliding and sin, all the while, tearing away at one's faith and belief in self. As the conflicting mindset of the devil and angel mentality ensues, the war of the mind and heart's battle for the soul begins, making the believer's path toward God a mostly uphill journey. As the deception and distorted worldview lay the foundation for a spiritual viewpoint, it is fair to say that the spiritual baby's comprehension, apprehension, trust, belief, and understanding of God's love and authority has been tainted by the preconceived notion of man's love and authority. Henceforth, obstructing one's ability to trust the forgiveness, unconditional love, and power of unseen God in the midst of so much physical pain, suffering, and betrayal, it very important to remember that the spirit of addiction has reared its ugly head in many different forms and through many different people. Although many will continue living in denial, many will identify this sickness of heart and mind as they release it to be nailed to the cross with Jesus Christ.

The point of examining this pivotal period in my life is to return to my past traumas in efforts to reassess the debilitating situations with an eye and mind of wisdom—the wisdom in knowing the results of how one's choices are certain to bare unwanted consequences, hopefully allowing the grace of choosing wisely in present and future endeavors. The relevance in knowing who and what you are as a whole will be the guiding instrument of light that leads to complete balance. Identifying as body, mind, and spirit requires one to understand their differences and what healing in these specific areas entail, henceforth creating a wholeness within the boundaries of one's own temple, which will in turn stimulate an understanding of wholeness in spiritual discernment.

It is of absolute importance that we have patience with ourselves and all others because we have no idea what our judgment and unenlightenment can create in the lives of God's already suffering children. There are those in our midst whose mental growth and development have been trampled by abuse, addiction, and/or physical or psychological brain trauma. Whether it was by force or choice, it is not our place as God's children to ignore, taunt, or condemn. Scripture tells us that we must be careful because the way in which we judge others is the same way in which we too shall be judged. It is so easy to become distracted away from one's own journey with the delusion of healing another person's flaws and sinful nature. God tells us to be thankful for all things—good and bad. What I did not know then was that all the choices and mistakes that I literally punished and imprisoned myself with through isolation, fear, shame, and guilt would be the same impactful testimony and healing tools used by the Holy Spirit in the lives of others that followed similar paths. For some reason, God created me to always see the light at the end of the tunnel. I truly believe that one small flicker of light could guide many out of the dark lonely places that sin dumps you. We must be careful when approaching others in judgment based on physical appearance and economic stature because although some may appear to be a certain age physically, they may not be that age psychologically. As a result of the stagnation of their mental capacity, they may not understand at an age-appropriate level yet. Working with the foster care and respite systems of our society has taught me that you have to meet people where they are, not where you think that they should be based on your timing and belief.

Meanwhile, we are called to follow the example of Christ's love and forgiveness with one another. The clearest sign that someone truly loves God is that they love people. As Christians, we are called to be loving toward our brothers and sisters in Christ and otherwise because our bond is what strengthens our faith. We are also called to be loving people of the world because it is our love that will be an example for them.

Inasmuch as I have contemplated who I am not, it would be impossible to move forward without knowing who I am now. So if I am no longer the manipulative, deceitful, gangbanging, drug, and alcoholic quitter, then who am I now? If I am no longer what others say that I am, then who am I now? If I am no longer the felon that the modern-day scarlet letter says that I am, then who am I now? If I am no longer what the medical specialist say that I am after seventeen major surgeries, then who am I now? If I am no longer what the generational curses say that I am, then who am I now? One thing for certain is that the only way that I will know who I am now would be to get to know who I am and whose I am.

The Gospel of Matthew introduces us to the incarnation and the preparation of the King, Jesus Christ. This book notes the declaration, manifestation and opposition of the King.

"[12]Scripture defines the Lord Jesus's royal aspect and career in Matthew. Not only was a descended from royal stock, but in infancy, He was also the recipient of gifts such as would be given to a king gold, frankincense, and myrrh (2:11). His famous 'Sermon on the Mount' was really the inaugural address of a King, embodying the essential principles of a new policy. His conflict with evil was the clash of two antagonistic kingdoms (12:26, 27). The parables of chapter 13 are the 'Transfiguration' was a sample of the Son of Man coming into His kingdom (16:28, 17:1–2), and from transfigura-

---

[12] Stanley D. Toussaint, *Behold the King*, "Theme of the Book," page 21.

tion to the passion in Jerusalem, Jesus proclaimed insistently that He would come again 'in His kingdom' (20:20–23, 25:31–46)."

We are now a new creature in Christ, which means that we have now become the cherished sons and daughters of God.

This means that we are no longer dominated by our sinful nature but are now controlled by the Holy Spirit because we have the Spirit of the living God's unconditional love, forgiveness, salvation, redemption, grace, and mercy dwelling inside of us with every breath we take.

Second Corinthians 5:17 explains, "Therefore, if anyone in Christ, he is a new creation, the old has gone, the new has come." The word "therefore" refers us back to versus 14 to 16 where Paul tells us that all believers have died with Christ and no longer live for themselves. Our lives are no longer worldly; they are now spiritual. Our death is that of the old sin nature, which was nailed to the cross with Christ. It was buried with Him, and just as He was raised up by the Father, so are we raised up to walk in the newness of life (Romans 6:4). The new person that Paul speaks of is what you are now—a new creation!

Dear God, I ask that in everything that I do, may I express the love You have for Your children and the world. May I never be tempted to become judgmental toward anyone. I ask that I will only be concerned with loving everyone around me. I pray for all those whom are suffering with an addictive mind and heart that God grace You with the peace, comfort, and wisdom that surpass all understanding. I ask that our spirit and mind be quickened. Touch our anxious hearts and calm the storm within with the spirit of acceptance and contentment. And, God, please allow me the faith and strength to stand in the belief and fullness of who You created me to be. I pray for the forgiveness for those who have attempted to create doubt in me of who I am and whose I am, in Jesus Christ's name, amen.

FASTING, PRAYER, AND MEDITATION

Tears poured from my eyes as chills engulfed my entire body. As I repeatedly tried to regain a standing position, my torso continued to thrust toward the tan plush carpet that covered the floors of my luxury apartment. I had no idea that the spirit of repentance had fallen upon my mind, heart, and body. This was a totally unexpected experience. Afterall, it was day thirty-nine of my first forty day shut in fast. I had completely reached the end of my road. I realize now that this period of my life was the third pivotal point in my journey. I was thirty-five years of age and had begun to experience the karmic consequences of my sinful choices and actions. I believe that fasting and prayer work hand in hand with each other. Otherwise, I was simply on a hunger strike. The point of fasting for me was to sacrifice what I deemed as earthly needs in order to focus more on communing with God. Prayer is how I commune with God during my time of fellowship.

Meditation is the technique that I use to silence the world's noises so that I am then able to hear what spirit has to say regarding my prayer request. It is at those times that I have received visions, revelations of God's word, and His goodness. It is easy to point the finger for your choices. However, the twelve steps of Alcoholics and Narcotics Anonymous has taught me that I have caused more destruction and harm to myself than any other person on the planet. My mental and physical growth and development have been stagnated by the choices that I made to cope with hurt, abandonment, abuse, and fear, which further stagnated my ability to comprehend spiritual concepts, interpretations, and directions at a spiritual age-appropriate level. These character defects cannot be removed by force or my sheer willpower, just as I cannot remove other people's character flaws with abusive insults, condemnation, or judgment.

My history of dealing with condemnation is to rebel. I bite off my nose to despite my face. The power and might of the Holy Spirit cannot be used to yield attacks on others that you feel has disrespected or hurt you in some way. People will attempt to use God as their personal hit man. They truly want God to overcome evil with evil. This is why I feel as though we should start with the Lord's Prayer because our pain and hurt may cause a distortion in one's thinking and prayer life. How can I lead myself in prayer when I have no idea of what the timing and will of God may be for any given situation? In addition to not having a clue of what could bring about true and lasting happiness, healing, or peace, most of the desires that I prayed for or touched and agreed again upon were the very things that eventually made me miserable. I believe that God allowed these manifestations in my life to teach me that I had no idea of what would make me happy or bring about peace. We tend to know the glory of a thing without knowing the story of what it took to manifest and maintain. That house that I prayed for was the same house that I would pull up at day after day and refuse to go inside because of stress and anxiety tied to it. The job that I touched and agreed with others to have is the same job that makes my daily reality unbearable. The husband that I verbally spoke into existence was the same husband that physically and verbally abused me on a daily basis, leaving me returning to God time and time again in hopes of having the very things that I asked for to be removed. For this reason, I have learned to contemplate these words daily in every choice that I make and in all that I do.

> But seek ye first the kingdom of God, and His righteousness, and all things shall be added unto you. (Matthew 6:33)

I had moved to a small town in Maryland to get away from the people, places, and things that my obsessive and compulsive disorder fixated on daily. The alcohol, cigarettes, gambling, and drugs resulting from the disease of addiction were the surface expressions of the inner turmoil. The fellowship of AA and NA call this being "a dressed-up garbage can." It is an overwhelming thirst for harmful things that never seem to be quenched. Fixation on harmful people, places, or things will begin the obsessive-compulsive desires that will steal the peace and vitality from one's self and all those they engage. I have often wondered why the desires of addiction have to all be harmful. Why not obsess over healthy, joyful things? The problem with running is that you will always take yourself and your thinking with you wherever you go. This period also represents when I stopped asking God for things as it relates to what I thought was best for my life, whether an idea or physical belonging. I simply had no idea what was best for me or what would bring about lasting joy, happiness, peace, or contentment. I could no longer trust myself or my own thinking at this point.

As my mind played the deeds of all that I had done or not done, a calmness fell upon my entire being. I was too weak to pick myself up off the floor. I was contorted into the fetal position as a voice from within said, "Big issues for little people" repeatedly in my mind and heart. Afterward, the voice said, "You are to go forward in teaching others in this world to love, protect, and nurture God's children and to fear not because I will guide and protect your steps, for the kingdom of heaven is at hand." I continued to lie on the floor in contemplation as spiritual downloads filled my awareness. What did this all mean? Was God asking me to protect children after losing two children of my own? Where was the protection for my unborn children? The notion of my obsession in being a mother would hinder God's plan for my mission because my attentions would have been solely on my obsession, as of all other obsessions in my life. Once I have fixated on something or someone, I then have a one-track mind.

Henceforth, would I have truly spent the time and devotion that I have given to so many of God's children outside of my womb and bloodline if I had children of my own?

At the time, I was a licensed child care provider in my home and had always made it my business to keep children safe, even through my sedative excursions. This was clearly something else. I had always taken my dream and vision life seriously because all that God had shown me prior in dreams and visions had become a reality. The difference in prophetic dreams versus an ordinary dream is that prophetic dreams had a way of consuming your every waking thought until it becomes a reality in the conscious realm. I had been preoccupied with the daily dreams of water flooding the familiar neighborhoods of DC. Witnessing the realism of the Washington Monument and the United States capital floating past you on the fourteenth street bridge is terrifying in itself. At this point, I was overwhelmed because I had not been able to complete anything within my own power up to this junction in my life. The spirit of doubt and fear tempted to remind me that it was all in my mind. Also that bipolar and paranoid schizophrenia ran rampart in the bloodline.

After having the courage to tell those that I trusted about the experience, I was blatantly told that it must be a mistake because no parent would listen to a motherless woman's advice on children, God, or otherwise. It all became too much for me to comprehend because I had absolutely no guidance outside of the Spirit of God. I had not yet committed to the study of scripture outside of Sunday service. I had no idea of how the character of God dealt with the areas of missions, prophecy, dreams, or visions. The Bible became alive to me because when I would follow the voice that said to pick up the Bible and open it; I would always open it to a page that would specifically explain my present situation. Nonetheless, I continued to hear an encouraging voice state that "more will be revealed." Finally, the disrespectful, condemning voices of all that I had loved and trusted, which plagued my mind and heart, were silenced. Although I had not familiarized myself with scripture yet, I found much joy, comfort, and healing in gospel and praise music. I can praise God for hours. It reminds me of how God loves us all. In addition to bringing about psychological and physical pain relief, God's word through song becomes imprinted in one's mind and heart. When scary and stressful situations surfaced in my daily life, I would hear God's word through divinely guided songs, which would shift the negative to a positive.

LOVING AND FORGIVING ONE'S SELF

"[13]Most young adults ages eighteen and over will move into adult roles and responsibilities and may learn a trade, work, and/or pursue higher education. Fully understand abstract concepts and be aware of consequences and personal limitations. Identify goals and prepare to achieve them. Early middle ages from thirty-five through forty-four should adhere to the emotional and developmental model, whereas, so little is normal, socially acceptable, and highly diverse in timing and order across individuals. Exposure to multiple viewpoints encourages development of a more complex self-concept that includes awareness of their own changing traits and values over time, along with enhanced self-esteem."

According to the young adult stages of development model, I am not where I should be developmentally due to my continued use of substances that impede psychological and physical brain development, which further stagnates one's emotional maturity, which has resulted in my inability to understand and act upon the basic understanding of forgiveness, salvation, and unconditional love. I am unable to give myself the forgiveness, trust, empathy, unconditional love, and understanding that I demand from others. The problem is that I do not trust forgiveness. My lifelong example of forgiveness has been tainted with the human condition. The forgiveness that I have witnessed came with emotional strings attached, depending on the forgiver's mood and temperament—meaning, as long as I am happy

---

[13] Galambos, Barker, Krahn. *Stages of Adulthood*, 2006; Montgomery & Cote 2003.

with you, all is forgiven. However, the moment that you upset me, I have the right to throw all that I had been forgiven back into your face, in most cases, as an attack of your character and walk with God. The hurtful, viciousness of such a demeaning attack from those that you have confided through being vulnerable will cause scarring on the minds and hearts of a young believer, *a baby* in Christ, and will surely limit their ability to understand God's forgiveness. This programming and brainwashing have not only taught us to condemn others through the inability to forgive; it has also caused us to turn this doubt and condemnation inward, which will attempt to stagnate kingdom growth because how could I offer forgiveness and unconditional love to others if I cannot stand in this intimate concept and notion myself. The good news is that the power, might, and will of the Holy Spirit is not dictated to by others' lack of wisdom and knowledge. The concept of "I can forgive but not forget" can no longer be used as an excuse to not follow the example of Jesus Christ's forgiveness toward us individually. The redemptive power of the holy Trinity has no limits or boundaries based on our fear and uncertainty. God has the power to brainwash the brainwashed. His healing and resurrecting power can restore what has been taken and rebuild what has been destroyed.

Micah 7:19 states, "He will turn again, He will have compassion upon us; He will subdue our iniquities; and thou wilt cast all their sins into the depths of the sea," better known as the "sea of forgetfulness."

Inasmuch as the conception of forgiveness seems out of reach, the inclination of love seems even further out of our grasp, primarily because of the various interpretations and examples of physical love. Love has been reduced to a whimsical desire and impulse of the imagination induced by a state of lust. I recall having a family discussion after Thanksgiving dinner with family and friends whereas my mother called me out in front of everyone. She asked me why I would ever continue to be around a person that would verbally and physically abuse me because this had not been her example and that we had never seen anyone put their hands on her. After sitting in awe for a moment, unbelievably shocked that this was the opening topic of discussion amongst people that I had not seen in years, I respectfully responded by asking my mother what the difference was in her verbally insulting me and/or hitting me because I failed to understand or act upon her demands, after which I was required to forgive and move forward with an understanding of why the disciplinary action was deemed necessary, as well as the fear and uncertainty of it repeating if I had further comprehension issues in the future. To come into someone's bedroom with alcohol pads to medically treat all the hot wheel track and leather belt welts covering their light-complected skin tone, with comforting words such as, "I did this because I love you and want what's best for you" as an apology might leave a distorted impression of love and protection in the young mind and heart of those that you are molding and shaping. Going forward it may also program one's thinking and behavior as it pertains to giving and receiving love. This misinterpretation of the character of love may even cause a person to feel unloved without violent, impulsive temperaments leading the way. History has shown us the results of what systemic, abusive measures has done to the mind and will of animals, countries, and historical figures alike. Can you imagine what it has and will do to the heart and mind of a repenting soul early in their walk with Christ? Such a stance can only yield confusion and distortions of what true love is and is not.

In Scriptures, love appears on every page and is what binds people together against dishonesty and hatred. In Christianity, agape is considered to be the love originating from God and Christ for humankind. God's first commandment to His people is to "love the Lord thy God with all thy heart, and with thy soul, and with all thy mind." And the second is to "love thy neighbor as you would yourself."

> [14]Love is patient, love is kind. It does not envy, it does not boast, it is not proud. It does not dishonor others, it is not easily angered, it keeps no record of wrongs. Love does not delight in evil

---

[14] *MacArthur Study Bible*, "Love," 1 Corinthians 13:4–6.

but rejoices with the truth. It always protects, always trusts, always hopes, and always perseveres. (1 Corinthians 13:4–6)

I believe that being critical of self and others is a total waste of time because people know what their struggles and issues are and, in most cases, are very critical of themselves without outside viewpoints. I have never seen or had an experience whereas the act of ridiculing, embarrassing, or shaming someone has produced positive and lasting results in behavior modification.

Nonetheless, this stage in my journey requires self-care and forgiveness. Allowing God to create a harmonic union between my body, mind, and soul is not as easy as I thought it would be. The wisdom bestowed upon the fifty-five-year-old today would tell the thirty-five-year-old me of yesterday that allowing God to create a balance is an absolute must. Once you have given your life to the Holy Spirit's process of redemption, you cannot stop those wheels from turning. What I realize now is that, as a young person, I felt physically invincible. However, I had to wrestle with the mind's balance of conscious and unconscious encounters and concepts. Whereas, I now have peace and contentment of mind, but my physical state is in need of balance through holistic care and restoration. At some point, they both have to be addressed and realized as a kingdom promise in the quest to love yourself as you would others. Although it is understood that hurt people hurt, and loved people love, it is not acceptable behavior before the throne. We belong to God. We are His children. Whenever the enemy tries to tell you otherwise, stand firm on God's word and remind the enemy of whom you belong to—God the Father. I just want to say thank you to God that I have my identity in Him, as His child. And I pray that when anyone tries to make me doubt who I am, I will simply shake them off and tell them confidently that I belong to You in Jesus's name. Amen.

Isaiah 43:1 states, "But now thus saith the Lord that created thee, O' Jacob and He that formed thee, O' Israel, fear not, for I have redeemed thee, I have called thee by thy name: thou art mine."

Wow! My Father's omnipotence, omnipresence, and omniscience are undeniable, and what's required of my heart is simply to believe this!—the faith of a mustard seed, one of the smallest seeds on earth. Amen!

A RENEWING OF THE MIND

As the sun rose on the last day of my forty-day fast, my mind became consumed with humility, truly wondering where I would go from that point. Remember, I had been living a looped life, doing the same things, expecting different results. I felt like a caged hamster running endlessly on a spinning wheel that was going nowhere, all the while, dealing with severe anxiety due to my claustrophobic mindset. I was often teased as a child because my feet felt trapped wearing shoes or being tucked in a bed. For the most part, I had drawn all of my fears directly to me. I had a fear of knives or being stabbed. I have had to endure seventeen major surgeries, which meant seventeen incisions by a blade. I have a fear of falling, and I find myself continually getting up from falling in life. Although I lose my mind in confined spaces, I have spent my entire adult life living in a locked up and confined mindset of being addicted to people, places, things, and beliefs. As I said earlier, I have no idea of what will provide the illusion of happiness. For this reason, I will make every effort not to lean on my understanding and strength.

The first mistake that I made after the anointing of the Holy Spirit fell upon me was to seek the guidance and wisdom of everybody but God concerning what I perceived as a mission called forward by the Almighty. I had no prior personal or professional experience or education in the field of parent education or child protection. After consulting with family and church members about what I had experienced and what God was telling me to do, I accepted the realization of it all being the arrogance of my ego. Why would God, in His glory, visit a barren, addicted, high school dropout, plagued by manipulation and deceit that never completed anything but running away. At least that is what those I cared for thought of me and had no problem sharing it with all who listened. However, the God that we serve will always follow through, even when others will not. His redemption has a way of showing up and showing out before all who dare to doubt His might. I had no idea that God had already put His plan for my life into motion. My mother's next-door neighbor, who we have known for ten years or so, was a director for a local teen parent and independent living program facility two blocks away in the neighborhood where I grew up. This was also the neighbor that had witnessed my extremely rebellious and sinful nature. She said that she also witnessed my empathy and compassion toward other suffering souls in the streets. She approached me a week after the completion of my fast at the corner store while I was visiting my mother. She explained that she was looking for a primary counselor to work the four to midnight shift, whereas they would have the opportunity to establish a relationship with the young mothers because they are usually home with their children during those hours. She further explained that these young women had all been severely abused and abandoned by their birth mothers and fathers as a result of the crack epidemic.

A month after accepting the position, I realized that when God calls you forward to work in His kingdom, one does not have to spin out of control, wondering how it will manifest. All that is required is simply faith and belief that it was real and that God will open the doors necessary for His will to be done.

In addition to being used to love, protect, and nurture the hurt and abandoned youth of our society, those same individuals were used to heal my broken heart of losing my children and not being able to have others. I loved this job as much as breathing. None of the long hours comforting their broken hearts, wiping away oceans of tears, sitting at children's hospital overnight, attending PTA meetings, and weekly vocational and psychological sessions bothered me in the least. Being exhausted did not compare to the smiles on their faces or the relief in their hearts as healing ensued. With patience, God will make it all make sense. I was offering and receiving unconditional love for the first time in my life. In the process of the Lord renewing my mind, other believer's minds were renewed as well.

HIS WILL BE DONE

Inasmuch as I was perfect for this job, it was perfect for me also. Unlike most of those that I worked with that approached the job with collegiate theory alone, I was unafraid to visit the ghettos and its residents to show empathy and compassion because I personally knew their suffering and their communities. It made my repentance real. I was able to go back to the people and neighborhood that I had helped to destroy as a vessel and a servant for the Lord's grace and mercy. As time went on, the job became a career that I took pride in, a career that provided the education and training that bought about a healing in me and those that I served. What began as a passion toward the youth grew into caring for the homeless, elderly, and mental-health population as well. I went places that racism and fear would not allow others to go. I guess having the blood of the African, the Native American, and the European gave the appearance of fitting in without a heart of judgment. Fighting the civil war within removes the need to fight it outside of myself. I am truly a melting pot of God's people and love.

The world around us is moving at an extremely fast pace. Subtle and blatant distractions are everywhere. We have become mesmerized with the realities of others, coveting our neighbor's lifestyle with an eye of curiosity, judgment, and lust, being programmed through mass media to focus on the excitement of the negatives. Afterall, negative behavior has always commanded attention and reaped vast rewards. This signals that we are attempting to distract ourselves away from the realities of our own lives, mistakes, pain, regret, guilt, and shame. We all know the distraction game. If I keep the focus on others, no one looks at me. Although it is important to identify the character flaws and defects that may have led to sinful behavior, it is also very important to acknowledge your good qualities and strengths. I personally see the glass as half full. However, that thought process took time to implement. Alone time with God is a must for spiritual grounding and awareness. Shutting out and turning off the world may seem scary at first because it is all that you know. Remember that this will help you to open the lines of communication between you and the holy Trinity.

The world that we live in was forged on the give-and-take system. We are often told that we have to earn all that we receive, which tempts us to believe that God's system works the same way, and there is something that we can do to purchase, barter, or earn forgiveness, salvation, or grace. This belief is so far from the truth. God desires faith and faith alone, which will undoubtedly lead to action commanded by His divine will and timing. The gifts and assignments that God has revealed to our hearts should be protected, treasured, and held in the highest regard, regardless of what others say, think, or believe. This is between you and the Most High. Getting to know who you are in God, as well as His character in all of His splendor and glory, will fill you with His transcendent love. His love will become so deeply rooted into your daily existence that it will begin to shine the light on situations and people that will offer the delusion of love.

Oftentimes we apply so much pressure to other people's lives by demanding them to be a soul mate. A soul mate is perceived as a force that will protect, provide, forgive, love unconditionally, and are at all places for you at all times. Based on these requirements, there are no human beings that I am aware of who fits this bill. For this reason, I believe that the Holy Spirit is and has always been my soul mate since conception into this realm. My spouse is my life companion and twin flame. Whereas, we both rely upon God for soul mate love. The Holy Spirit alone has the might and ability to know all things, *omniscience*; always present in time of need, *omnipresence*; and powerful in every situation that life has for you, *omnipotent*. When I think about it, my companion was not able to be there when my legs gave away and I fell down a flight of stairs, breaking my back and neck, nor was he able to guide the hands of either of the seventeen surgeons that worked to save my life and so forth. Once we accepted the perspective that it was not another human being's job to heal, comfort, or provide, our relationship was graced with the peace, joy, and the excitement that stress diminishes. I found that turning to God with life's concerns and stresses, instead of adding more burden to someone else that is just as overwhelmed as I am, creates an example that we both can rest in. People in this world are already drowning in hurt, fear, loss, and frustration; why then would one want to add the straw that may break the camel's back? When we accept God as our soul mate, we learn to lean not on our own understanding, which is a major act of faith.

God's love renewed my mind by way of His commanding words, timing, and will. I received that renewing through faith alone. That faith led to the action and deeds of moving in the spirit as a kingdom representative.

REDEMPTION

"[15]Praise be to the God and Father of our Lord Jesus Christ who has blessed us in heavenly realms with every spiritual blessing in Christ. For He chose us in Him before the creation of the world to be holy and blameless in His sight. In love, He predestined us for adoption to sonship through Jesus Christ, in accordance with His pleasure and will to the praise of His glorious grace, which He has freely given us in the One He loves. In Him, we have redemption through His blood, the forgiveness of sins, in accordance with the riches of God's grace that He lavished on us. With all wisdom and understanding, He made known to us the mystery of His will according to His good pleasure, which He purposed in Christ to be put into effect when times reach their fulfillment to bring unity to all things in heaven and on earth under Christ" (Ephesians 1:3–10).

"[16]The underlying theme of all the Scriptures is redemption—in the Old Testament, the anticipation of it in type and prophecy; in the gospels, the accomplishment of it by the death of Christ; in Acts and Epistles, the application of it to the needs of man; and in the Revelation, the achievement of it in the subjection of all kingdoms to the rule of God. As running through all British Navy rope, there is a thread of some color according to the dockyard in which it is made, so running through all the Scriptures is the saving purpose, making the whole Bible an unfolding drama of redemption. Into this drama, all the details fit at each stage of its unfolding, so that each and every part of the Bible, whether history or literature or type or

---

[15] *The MacArthur Study Bible*, "Redemption," Ephesians 1:3–10.

[16] W. Graham Scroggie, *The Unfolding Drama of Redemption*, "Redemption in the Bible," p. 32.

prophecy or law or grace is the part of the design of God to reconcile to Himself by the sacrifice of Himself, a fallen and rebellious race. In the thought of many, a drama is simply a theatrical entertainment. But such an idea misses the essential meaning of the word and may be destructive of it. What is common to the theatrical and the dramatic is action. But in the former, the action is feigned. And in the latter, it is real; it is actual, not artificial; it is a living scene and not a mere semblance. Human history, regarded as a whole, is a drama setting forth the struggle of the human mind with life's dark problems and emotions, the conflict of faith and doubt, of joy and sorrow, of hope and despair."

The gift of redemption has been a gradual process as it pertains to my life. I know that some believe they received complete redemption the day that they surrendered to salvation; but for most believers, it is a lifelong process. God is continually bestowing His gift of redemption as I live, learn, and attempt to dodge the alluring pitfalls of this world. The Holy Spirit's process of redemption has begun the restoration process of my mind, heart, and body—the mind's perceptions, words, and understanding; the heart's fears, hurts, resentments, grief, and lustful temptations; and the body's diet, stress, pains, unhealthy cravings, and physical ailments, such as diseases. An individual believer's process of redemption does not depend on another person's desire to see you change or in their timing. The mind, heart, and body's redemption process has allowed the balance that is required to comprehend intuition and the discernment of the divine will and promise of God in my journey toward realizing a balanced Christian walk with the assistance of the Holy Spirit's guidance, encouragement. and power.

SPIRITUAL GIFTS REVEALED

It was six in the evening, and I found myself standing at the crosswalk of the intersection of Southern Avenue and Wheeler Road in Southeast DC. As the sun began to set on the day, I simply stood there, feeling dazed and confused. The traffic light's rotation from red to green and then to yellow pulled me into a hypnotic state. As a trance-like state engulfed my mind, my feet felt as though I was wearing concrete shoes. I felt like time was standing still because there was absolutely no movement from the people or vehicles that surrounded me. As I continued to peer in the direction of Wheeler Road, anxiety overwhelmed me at the sight of the wall of water headed toward me. As the filthy water consumed everything in its path, people started screaming and running frantically in every direction. I became paralyzed with fear. My first thought was to grab the huge light post beside me on the corner. I did just that! I wrapped my arms around the large wooden pole as the murky water with all sorts of debris slammed into my back. The water surrounded me with at least the height of fifteen feet. My eyes remained open the entire time to witness the dead bodies and totally lost vehicles swirling by at an enormous speed. I began choking as the water filled my nose and mouth. I recall trembling uncontrollably in horror as the taste of raw sewage tantalized my taste buds. Apparently, I passed out because the next thing that I remember was waking up in the aftermath. Although the water had begun to recede, garbage, junk, debris, and disheveled people were everywhere. Survivors were in search of loved ones and some sense of familiarity. I did not understand why men, women, and children were flocking to me for help. As their cries for help pulled me out of the trance state that loomed, I was then able to comprehend my environment and what was being asked of me. The crazy thing is that those strangers had no idea that I was a family support specialist that assisted individuals in time of crisis. The wisdom of my case management skills kicked in and shifted into high gear. I started to organize the chaos with prayer, humility, empathy, and encouragement, which resulted in getting God's children to safety and back in the arms of their loved ones.

When I woke up and realized that the whole saga was a dream with the realism of me still having the taste of sewage in my mouth, I crawled from the bed to my knees with fear and trembling because this was one of those unshakable dreams that fell into the prophetic category. For seven days, this dream was all that I could think of until I arrived at the family support collaborative for work, and my supervisor walked into the daily case management meeting with tears in her eyes, stating that hurricane Katrina hit New Orleans, and a large number of survivors would be arriving and receiving care and assistance at the Stadium Army. I found myself standing in the dream that I had seven days prior. After months of assisting hundreds of hurt, afraid, and displaced people in finding psychological care and treatment, housing, financial assistance, and lost loved ones, the dream and taste in my mouth slowly subsided.

LOVING THY NEIGHBOR

I have always loved people. It does not matter what the race, age, gender, religious biases and beliefs, or lifestyle. I embrace living and engaging a variety of races and their cultures. I have learned a great deal from them all. I have always been approachable, just as I have no problem approaching others in a loving and respectable manner. I have learned to meet and accept people for who and where they are or want to be. When I am blessed with the opportunity to commune with others, I do not waste time with debates, pointing fingers, or judgment. Working with children of all ages taught me that a college student would never argue with a preschooler about life or beliefs. After planting the seeds of the spirit, I believe that it will take root in God's timing and process. And one day, it will all make sense to them. I am convinced that the same God that loves, protects, and guide my steps has the power to do the same in the lives of others. Although God may have selected me to plant the seeds, He may have something or someone else in mind for the watering and harvest process.

As a matter of fact, I have always assisted my family and community by way of babysitting for family, friends, and neighbors and helping the elderly with shopping, housekeeping, running errands, and companionship. Much to my surprise, most of my friends would be considered senior citizens. My grandmothers were literally my best friends. It is probably because I enjoyed the wisdom in their heroic and inspirational stories about life. A pearl of wisdom was shared with me during every visit. I would listen in awe of their ability to adapt and endure in a rapidly changing body and world. It is fair to say that I enjoyed community social work long before there were paychecks involved.

God has inspired so many resource-based programs to assist the family and community as a whole. The problem with so many is that loving thy neighbor requires them to confront evil sometimes. After witnessing the evil that came with a lifestyle of addiction and the horrors that people inflict on one another through adult and child protection, one has to be grounded in more than just physical well-being. Forgiveness, unconditional love, gratitude, empathy, compassion, trust, and the wisdom to face some of the most evil in this world without bias must adhere to constant fasting and prayer for divine guidance, courage, and protection. Once I understood the propensities of generational curses and that most people did not believe that their family curses died with Jesus at the cross, I was equipped and able to assist both the abused and the abuser. The ability to love those that society has deemed the unlovable or those that have done the same thing to others that was done to me is a testament and example of God's love and redemption in action.

> [17]Jesus went into the mount of Olives. And early in the morning, He came again unto the temple, and all the people came unto Him; and He sat down and taught them. And the scribes and Pharisees brought unto Him a woman taken in adultery; and when they had sat her the midst, they say unto Him, Master, this woman was taken in adultery in the very act. Now Moses in the law commanded us that such should be stoned: but what sayest thou? This they said, tempting Him, that they might have to accuse Him. But Jesus stooped down and, with His finger, wrote on the ground, as though He heard them not. So when they continued asking Him, He lifted up Himself and said unto them, He who is without sin among you, let him first cast a stone at her. And again, He stooped down and wrote on

---

[17] *The MacArthur Study Bible*, "Casting the First Stone," John 8:1–12.

the ground. And they which heard it, being convicted by their own conscience, went out one by one, beginning at the eldest, even unto the last; and Jesus was left alone and the women standing in the midst. When Jesus had lifted up Himself and saw none but the woman, he said unto her, woman, where are these thine accusers? Hath, no man condemned thee? She said, no man, Lord. And Jesus said unto her, neither do I condemn thee: go and sin no more. Then spake Jesus again unto them, saying, I am the light of the world: he that followeth Me shall not walk in darkness but shall have the light of life. (John 8:1–12).

THE PEACE IN LETTING
GO AND LETTING GOD

I am forty-five years old, and I believe that this time in my life is representative of the fourth pivotal point in my journey toward realizing a balanced Christian walk. God finally blessed me with the love of my life. His love for spirit ignited our love and has sustained our twin flame for ten years now. It is absolutely refreshing to have a life companion that allows God to guide us both. He does not have or waste time trying to change the very things that he fell in love with. We fast, pray, worship, and praise together as a family. Our union has graced me with a huge family that love and honor God and marriage. God understands my love for the elderly in my family. And although both of my grandmothers have transcended, He gave my husband's grandmother, Grandma Hawk. I instantly fell in love with her grace, beauty, patience, wisdom, and love for family and God. She nicknamed me Ladybug. What an honor!

I have continued to fast in prayer through hardships. I feel as though I have matured in some ways; however, God is still molding and shaping my way. The struggle through an addictive mindset has been real. It causes problems with my ability to completely let go.

The most difficult thing has been to let go of a particular mindset, especially regarding a diet adopted through family traditions. Inasmuch as our diet has been accepted as a delicious comfort food, it has wreaked havoc on my loved one's health and well-being. Just as I have had to let go of harmful substances and people, cultivating a healthy diet is imperative for both the brain and body. During my time of sickness and suffering, I was unable to focus or discern the will of God in my life or offer kindness in the midst of severe nerve pain or healing surgical wounds. This was when I would often recite the serenity prayer, which asks God to "grant us the serenity to accept the things that we cannot change and the courage to change the things that we can and the wisdom to know the difference." This means that although I cannot change the traditional ancestry diet of yesterday, based on the results of what unhealthy eating has done to my bloodline for centuries, I can change my choices in diet today.

Instead of continually asking God to heal my temple, I have shifted that prayer to asking God for the wisdom to honor the temple the houses of the Holy Spirit, which makes our temples holy ground. Unlike the elders of our families, we have an overabundance of reliable information on the topic, and we have witnessed its results as our loved ones perish from a lack of knowledge as it pertains to unhealthy eating. Our freezers look like pet cemetery, and that is to say the least. Our highly parasitic diet has caused God's animals to endure some horrific challenges for the sake of a gourmet meal. The bad part of it is that most of the slaughtered animals are left on plates and thrown in the garbage. We have no idea of what it takes to get that animal from the farm to our plates. And with all the mega-sized grocery stores that have freezers and shelf food of alternate choices, unlike our ancestors, one would think that our health and death stats would have fallen.

I have to accept that my life is no longer my own and that God has a specific plan for every aspect of my life, including diet. It is so much easier to let go of the things that society has rendered evil, illegal, or unhealthy. However, it can be a bit challenging to walk away from what is acceptable, like liquor stores, smoking cigarettes, gambling, or dietary choices, which all play on our vulnerabilities, insecurities, and lack of knowledge.

Eventually, I reached a point that I could no longer continue to ask God to heal my temple and continue putting inflammatory, poisonous, and parasitic garbage in the temple of God. Once again, I kept eating the same things, expecting different results. That is the definition of insanity. Was I eating food, or was my food eating me?

The dreams of massive water engulfing areas began to extend beyond DC. The urgency in the weekly dreams of areas flooding has turned to an urgency of me getting to the middle. I was unsure of what that meant but just believed that more will be revealed.

The manifestations of the Spirit are to assist us as believers with our journey. In addition to the Holy Spirit's ability to produce Christian character and love, it teaches, leads, edifies, praises in thanksgiving, and Christian service while witnessing and making intercession for us.

When someone has surrendered to an idea, belief, or system, it is important that one conforms to its ideals. For example, if one has given themselves unto a life of crime and breaking man's laws, then they must comply and conform to the court system's idea of punishment or rehabilitation. And although one has never been locked up, they will quickly adapt to the prison mentality and lifestyle. The same goes with marriage, employment, housing, and so forth. A wife submits to her husband, an employee adheres to company policy, and residents follow the guidelines of their signed lease agreement.

What I have found at this point in my journey is that I have not completely submitted to the will and life of a Christian. My rebellious nature and strong will has attempted to deceive me into believing that I can accomplish kingdom goals without first knowing the word of God. Although I randomly study the Bible and can quote a few scriptures, I have yet to commit to digging deeper into the Old and New Testaments of God's divinely inspired word. I have entered the battle without a sword, which is the word of God. How can I begin to combat the day-to-day evil that attacks my life without knowing how the character of God has responded to similar situations throughout history?

I have heard the testimonies of scripture actually coming alive to those that open the book to feast upon its contents. What has fascinated me about the scriptures that I have studied is that it grows with you. So in a sense, it is alive, meaning that when I have read a particular scripture at age fifteen, it had a meaning that addressed that stage in life. When I read that same scripture at age twenty-five, it held a different meaning altogether based on my understanding during that stage. Just as reading that same scripture at thirty-five, forty-five, and so on.

Letting go and letting God requires the ability to trust. According to the adult stages of development, I am still underdeveloped because I should be able to grasp and comprehend the concepts of trust and faith. I have an abundance of quantity faith and a lack of quality faith. When I walk into a building or my home, I have faith that the walls, floors, and ceilings will sustain my shelter. When I drive a vehicle, I believe that it will get me safely to my destination. How then, after all that God has blessed me with, do I still wrestle with trusting His holy process of salvation and redemption, which entails "to study and shew thyself approved unto God." Why would it be considered less important than studying at medical school to be a doctor, or law school to be lawyer. Can you imagine your surgeon approaching heart surgery with no prior knowledge or study on the subject? Or facing life in prison with an attorney that never attended law school? Or approaching a person's spiritual demise or walk with Christ without first knowing His blueprint? A wise man once said that it is in the contract, the Bible, and we must read in its entirety. The Bible is that contractual agreement between God and His kingdom.

The old man has an Adamic nature, which was judged at the cross with the death of Jesus Christ. It still abides with us as an active participant in our lives. However, victory will be realized through reliance upon the Holy Spirit, which is equipped with the will and might of God our heavenly Father as it sustains our lives individually and collectively as His kingdom babies.

SPIRITUAL MATURITY AND ENLIGHTENMENT

It was a beautiful fall day, and I had chosen to sit in my mother-in-law's rose garden to watch the Sunday morning sunrise. As I sat in my robe and slippers, sipping a hot cup of hazelnut coffee, I was enamored at the blend of colors in the sky and all the wondrous nature that surrounds me in this moment. The gentle calmness of it all had bought me to tears. The sound of the birds chirping began to fade into a ringing noise in my ears, followed by a strange, loud buzzing frequency. When I opened my eyes, everything appeared to be blurred. What I was seeing did not seem real.

In addition to being startled, I was also frightened because strokes run in our family. When I attempted to stand, I felt as though I was moving in slow motion. I sat back down and began to slow down my breathing and recite the Lord's prayer out loud, as I always do in times of fear, anxiety, and stress. I sat in silence for quite a while after the prayer ended.

Out of nowhere, I began trembling throughout my entire body. As a calm and subtle voice said to fast in prayer without ceasing because something tragically terrible was about to happen on earth. "Brace yourself" chanted repeatedly in my heart and mind. Afterward, a tremendous feeling of sorrow and grief fell upon my consciousness. As the feeling began to fade away, I felt exhausted and overcome with need for sleep. I made my way inside, lay down, and fell asleep. When I woke up, I shared the experience with my husband and sister. They asked me what I thought it all meant. I had no reply other than I would be fasting about the fast. Somehow, fasting has always been instinctive to me. My mother said that she felt that the majority of her pregnancy was a forced fast because I would not allow her to hold anything down.

Meanwhile, my husband and I had to finish packing because we were moving to Dallas, Texas, and our flight was leaving at six in the morning.

As I peered from the window of the airplane in route to Dallas, Texas, a lot of thoughts flooded my mind, thoughts like being told to move to the middle after all of the flood dreams, and then circumstances arose that moved my family to Dallas, which was almost geographically in the middle of the map that I was looking at.

When I stepped off the plane in Dallas, I felt like I was home. Washington, DC, is the only other place that I have lived and felt the security of home. Two months after settling into my new home, life, and city, I was consumed with dreams of social unrest. Months later, I turned on the morning news to the coronavirus and possible shutdowns—talk about something horrific happening on earth, followed by immense sorrow and social unrest. I turned to another news broadcast, and there was catastrophic flooding around the world. It was a good thing that I was obedient in fasting and prayer, followed by an immune building diet. We all know what happens next! What also happened to me on a personal level was that I felt confirmed and closer to God than ever. All the ridicule that I have received over the years when sharing prophetic dreams with others became disheartening at times, not that I wanted these things to happen but that God saw fit to prepare us in advance. My dream's state is just as real to me as my waking state.

Today is my fifty-fifth birthday, and I am celebrating it with my adorable husband of twenty years. I am an honor student, completing the bachelor of art program at Tyndale Theological Seminary with focus on the Bible and theology. I received the Kay Courtney Courage and Devotion Award, which completely pays for school. I feel as though I have reached the fifth pivotal point in my journey. Finally, through the structure and discipline attained as result of my commitment to seminary bile study, I have begun to realize a balanced Christian walk. And although a global pandemic is horrific in itself, it has also been an opportunity for reflection and time to connect with God, self, and the family. I have noticed that people are no longer taking life for granted because we realize that tomorrow is never promised to any of us. I no longer do things expecting anything in return, nor do I distract myself with the day-to-day concerns that I have given to God for edification. I love and treat my neighbors with respect, hope, and encouragement, regardless of what they are able to offer me in return. I address each individual, no matter the race, age, gender, or lifestyle in manner in which Jesus Christ would have me to present myself as His representative. I continue to offer food, resources, and the good news of Christ to the homeless of my community. My fasting, study, and prayer life has grown tremendously. And I have learned the importance and honor of self-love and care. I am finally able to give myself the unconditional love, forgiveness, and physical pampering that has bought about an inexplicable joy, peace, love, and understanding of myself and the world in which I live. I am now able to accept life on life's terms without the use of sedative substances, solely relying on the wisdom and comfort of the Holy Spirit. And although my body continues to endure much pain and suffering as I embark on the aging process, I have found a natural balance in providing it with a wholesome diet, rest, and a relaxed state of mind and heart but often reminding myself that although we attempt to eat right and live a healthy lifestyle, eventually, one day this body will shut down, and we all will experience death.

The serenity payer and Lord's prayer continue to be the only prayers that I pray for self and others. And although I have lost an enormous amount of family, friends, and neighbors in such a short time, my grief has been turned into joy because I believe they are no longer tied to the hurt and suffering of this world. God's word reminds us that "we are confident, yes, well pleased rather to be absent from the body and to be present with the Lord" (2 Corinthians 5:8). Wow! Imagine that! No more physical or mental anguish, pain or suffering after having lived and experienced the joy and peace in a life of faith, patience, love, forgiveness, and devotion unto the Most High God!

BIBLE STUDY AND INTERPRETATIONS

God's divinely inspired word has introduced me to the character and commitment of God and has become a lifeline to a closer relationship with His Majesty. God's word has transformed my mind and heart's desires into honoring the will of God in my life and those that I serve. His word has afforded me a tool for research, discipline, and study. Whereas, I no longer rely upon the misinformation or misinterpretations of those that are yet to commit to an actual study of the divine word. God's word has also transformed and shielded my thoughts from the ravenous, repetitive nature of addiction that attempted to stunt my growth and comprehension. I no longer put unbearable pressure on other human beings for what can only be obtained in the Spirit. His word has taken root in my mind, which has blossomed in heart and walk with my Lord and Savior, inspiring an unquenchable faith and trust in Him!

> Study to shew thyself approved unto God, A
> workman that needeth not to be ashamed, rightly
> dividing the word of truth. (2 Timothy 2:15)

Biblical interpretations are very important with regard to understanding and teaching God's word. If we do not approach and interpret the Bible properly, we more than likely will begin to draw false conclusions regarding salvation, redemption, and all else in the scripture.

Although we are solely reliant upon the Holy Spirit for interpretation, it may be important for some to have a teacher or church to assist with interpretations, especially as a babe in Christ. This is why hermeneutics of the Bible is so important because we only have the Bible to tell us what to believe and how to live. And if that is misinterpreted, then everything that follows represents that belief. God's living word also has major functions: It testifies concerning Jesus Christ. John 5:39 states, "You search scripture because in them you have eternal life, and it is these that testify concerning Me." It offers the wisdom of salvation. Second Timothy 3:15 states, "And that from a babe you have known the sacred writings, which are able to make you wise unto salvation through the faith which is in Christ Jesus." It is regenerative. First Peter 1:23 states, "Having been regenerated not of corruptible, through the living and abiding word of God." It is spiritual milk for the believer. First Peter 2:2–3 states, "As newborn babies, long for the guileless milk of the word in order that by it you may grow unto salvation, if you have tasted that the lord is good." It is the believer's bread of life. Matthew 4:4 states, "It is written, 'Man shall not live on bread alone, but on every word that proceeds out of through the mouth of God." And it makes a believer complete. Second Timothy 3:16–17 states, "All scripture is God-breathed and profitable for teaching, for conviction, for correction, for instruction in righteousness, that the man of God may be complete, fully equipped for every good work."

THE BODY OF CHRIST

In Christianity, the term body of Christ has a two-part meaning. It is first defined as the prayer that Jesus did over the bread at Passover, "This is My body" in Luke 22:19–20, and it represents all individuals who are Christ (1 Corinthians 12:12–14). As the body of Christ, we are linked by the Spirit of God that runs through us all, henceforth, spirituality.

"[18] Genuine spirituality involves three factors. The first is regeneration. No one can be spiritual in the biblical sense without having first experienced the new life that is freely given to all who believe in the Lord Jesus Christ as personal Savior. Spirituality without regeneration is reformation. Second, the Holy Spirit is preeminently involved in producing spirituality. This is not to say that the other persons of the Godhead do not have a part in it, nor that the believer himself has no responsibility, nor that there are no other means of grace; but it is to affirm His major role in spirituality. The ministries of the Holy Spirit involve teaching (John 16:12–15), guiding (Romans 8:14), assuring (Romans 8:16), praying (Romans 8:26), and the exercise of spiritual gifts (1 Corinthians 12:7) and warring against the flesh (Galatians 5:17). The third factor involves time. If the spiritual person judges or examines or discerns all things (1 Corinthians 2:15), this must involve time in order to gain knowledge and to acquire experience for discerning all things. The Amplified Bible elaborates on the verse in this fashion: "He can read the meaning of everything, but no one can properly discern or appraise or get an insight into Him." This could not be accomplished overnight; it is something which is true only of a mature Christian. All of these

---

[18] Charles C. Ryrie, *Balancing the Christian Life*, "What is Spirituality," p. 12–13.

depend for their full manifestation on the filling of the Spirit. To be filled by the Spirit means to be controlled by the spirit."

What I realized going forward in the body of Christ is that His kingdom is all sufficient. Anything or anyone that you will ever need can be found within the body of Christ. We are your parents, children, siblings, extended family, pastors, teachers, prayer warriors, writers, doctors, lawyers, judges, carpenters, plumbers, brick layers, child care providers, artist of all kinds, housekeepers, gardeners, builders, businessmen and women, accountants, bus drivers, farmers, road workers, social workers, foster parents and children, psychological fields, healers, convicts, homeless people, mentally challenged, law enforcement, military, first responders, store clerks, stockers, maintenance, management, and denominational, as well as the nondenominational. We are many! It is also fair to say that anything that you are in need of can be found within the body of Christ, with an identification of words, such as praise or glory to God, and thank You, Jesus!

Inasmuch as God's plan for His children included an overabundance of resources outside of ourselves, He also has an angelic support system in place for our spiritual quest toward Him with the intention of growing in His image.

Archangels are represented throughout the Bible. They are classified as spiritual beings intermediate between God and men. In chapter 20 of Enoch, it mentions seven holy angels who watch and are considered to be the seven archangels: Michael, Raphael, Gabriel, Uriel, Selaphiel, Raguel, and Ramiel.

"[19]Believers say that God has assigned guardian angels to protect each individual person on earth, but He often sends archangels to accomplish earthly tasks of a larger scale. For example, the archangel Gabriel is known for his appearances delivering major messages to people throughout history. Christians believe that God sent Gabriel to inform the Virgin Mary that she would become the mother of Jesus Christ on earth. Michael represents the victory of good over

---

[19] Whitney Hopler, *Archangels: God's Leading Angels*, "Archangels," updated May 1, 2019, Defined@Learningreligions.com.

evil and protects and defends people who love God. Raphael represents the healing of the body, mind, and spirits. Gabriel represents God as His heavenly messenger. Uriel represents wisdom and truth. Selaphiel represents prayer and worship. Raguel represents justice, fairness, harmony, vengeance, and redemption. Ramiel represents hope and divine visions."

The most significant part of the Body of Christ is that Christ gave His body and blood according to His promise to all to partake, eating and drinking the body and blood of Christ with expectant faith, whereby we have communion with the body and blood of our Lord and Savior and receive the forgiveness of sins and receive life and salvation.

KINGDOM DISCIPLESHIP

Kingdom discipleship has been the process in which I fully submit to God with the intention and goal of building a strong relationship with Him, in the hopes of better serving His people and kingdom.

"[20]There is a call to believers to use the Word empowered by the Spirit to minister to one another. You, who are Christians, are competent to minister by the grace of God; you can care for souls. The care of souls depends upon all of the 'alones' of reformation by Scripture, grace, Christ, faith, and the glory of God alone. These principles apply to all aspects of salvation, including justification, sanctification, and glorification. Believers are to continue their walk with the Lord on the same basis as their initial salvation by Scripture alone, by grace alone, by Christ alone, by faith alone, and to the glory of God alone. All these apply within the individual life of the believer and within the body of Christ in which we have the fellowship and the priesthood of all believers. Mutual care within the body of Christ, performed by a priesthood of all believers also depends upon these same principles. We want to emphasize this at the very beginning because of the tenacious tendency to use other means for living a Christian life and solving problems of living."

Understanding that the kingdom is under God's reign, rule, and authority and as His disciple, one of my jobs is to disciple others and spread the good news of the holy Trinity, embracing the journey, kingdom life, and discipleship by living by faith in Christ, walking in the Spirit, and resting in God's grace.

---

[20] Martin and Deidra Bobgan, *Competent to Minister*, p. 4–5.

DEFENDING THE FAITH

There are so many hurt and frustrated people and believers alike that are tempted to be distracted with an eye and heart of judgment by what they perceive as another person's evil and sinful nature. Although we are called to pray for the sins of man, we are also called to have the faith in the God for that person's deliverance. Some even feel as though the omnipresence of God will not see the secrets of man's heart, mind, and deeds. There is no place on earth that we can hide from our Creator, just as Adam and Eve could not hide their rebellion in the garden of Eden nor can the abusive husband, the swindler, the misleading pastors, the cheating spouse, the murderer, the pedophile, the thief, or the fool that denies the existence of the holy Trinity.

It is not our job, as believers, to condemn, curse, persecute, dismiss, gossip, or damn the unenlightened among us to hell. Rather, we should offer the same love, kindness, gentleness, and empathy that was given to us by our the Lord Jesus Christ's forgiveness, unconditional love, grace, and mercy. Our example of love may be a nonbeliever's first encounter with God's representative.

"[21]The central declaration and challenge of Christian apologetics is expressed by Paul's rhetorical question: "Hath not God made foolish the wisdom of the world" (1 Corinthians 1:20). Critical attacks, which are leveled against the Christian faith in the world of thought, cannot be met by piecemeal replies and appeals to emotion. In the long run, the believer must respond to the onslaught of the unbeliever by attacking the unbeliever's position at its foundation. He must challenge the unbeliever's presuppositions, asking whether

---

[21] Dr. Greg L. Bahnsen, *Always Ready*, "The Foolishness of Unbelief," p. 55.

knowledge is even possible, given the non-Christian assumptions and perspective. The Christian cannot forever be defensively, constructing atomistic answers to the endless variety of unbelieving criticisms. He must take the offense and show the unbeliever that he has no intelligible place to stand, no consistent epistemology, no justification for meaningful discourse, predication, or argumentation. The pseudowisdom of the world must be reduced to foolishness, in which case, none of the unbeliever's criticisms have any force."

CONCLUSION

The journey from a Christian babe toward realizing a balanced Christian walk had been filled with forgiveness, unconditional love, empathy, strength, and enlightenment. When I prayed to God for His strength, wisdom, knowledge, peace, joy, love, and understanding, I had no idea that I would have to welcome the experiences that would bring it about. When asking for strength, one should be prepared to endure the task that will bring about strength and so forth.

I have met so many incredible people from all walks of life with fascinating testimonies of experience, strength, and hope. There is absolutely no way that anyone would have convinced me to believe that this would be my existence today. It is unfathomable that I am writing this book as a gift of hope and inspiration for the world. I believe that my life as God's vessel of service to His kingdom requires complete faith, trust, courage, and transparency before the kingdom and the kingdom babies alike. I ask God daily to decrease me so that He may be increased. The gift of spiritual growth and maturity came over time through the Holy Spirit's process of redemption and God's timing. As a believer matures, they will no longer fear the distractions of their surroundings, nor will they have to worry about generational curses or being psychologically or emotionally challenged due to choices made before salvation. The Holy Spirit will create the healing environment necessary for each believer through His love and intimacy. Be gentle and patient with one another and the kingdom babies because He specifically called them forward by name. Our life should be a shining example before all of His love.

It is important to remember that we are under the covenant of the New Testament's grace and mercy. And that sin can be its own judge, jury, and executioner. God is God all by Himself. And although it may get scary at times, we must trust that His power alone will balance your body, mind, and soul to the will of His Spirit. All that we need to do is trust Him through faith.

ENDNOTES

1. William R. Newell, *Romans, Verse by Verse.* Kregel Publications grand Rapids MI. Chapt. 10 pgs. 387-389
   ISBN: 978-0-8254-3339-9.
2. The American Society of Addiction. *Addiction Medicine.* Copyright 2019. All rights reserved ASAM.org
3. The MacArthur Study Bible. *The Lord's Prayer*, Matthew 6:9–13. 2006
4. Reinhold Neburhr. *The Serenity Prayer.* 1971–1982 nndb.com
5. Bill W. *The Big Book.* Alcoholics Anonymous. Published 1939. OCLC: 408888189.
6. The MacArthur Study Bible, *Temptation*, James 1:12–13.
7. The MacArthur Study Bible, *Conquerors*, Roman 8:37
8. The MacArthur Study Bible, *He Who is Greater.* 1 John 4;4.
9. Galambos, Barker and Krahn, *Stages of Adulthood.* 2006 Montgomery and Cote. Psycnet.apa.org
10. Katelyn Kleisinger. *Four types of Sin.* Prezi Inc. 2022. prezi.com
11. The MacArthur Study Bible. *Do not be overcome by evil.* Romans 12:21.
    Hawkins/THE BABE125
12. Stanley Toussaint. *Behold the King.* Theme of the book page 21. Kregel Publications Grand Rapids MI. 1980. ISBN: 978-0-8254-3845-5.
13. Galambos, Barker, and Krahn. *Stages of Adulthood.* 2003. psycnet.apa.org
14. The MacArthur Study Bible. *Love.* 1 Corinthians 13:4–6.
15. The MacArthur Study Bible. *Redemption,* Ephesians 1:3–1.

16. W. Graham Scroggie. *The Unfolding Drama of Redemption.* Redemption in the Bible p. 32. Kregel Publications Grand Rapids MI. 1994. ISBN: 978-0-8254-3774-8.

17. The MacArthur Study Bible. *Casting the first stone,* John 8:1–12.

18. Charles C. Ryrie. *Balancing the Christian Life.* What is Spirituality pgs. 12–13. Moody Publishers Chicago IL. ISBN: 978-0-8024-0887-7.

19. Whitney Hopler. *Archangels: God's Leading Angels.* defined@ learningreligions.com, updated 2019.

20. Martin and Deidra Bobgan. *Competent to Minister.* Pgs. 4–5. East gate Publishers, Santa Barbara CA. 1996. ISBN: 0-941717-11-9.

21. Dr. Greg L. Brahnsen. *Always Ready.* The Foolishness of Unbelief, P.55. Covenant Media Press. Nacogdoches TX. 1996. ISBN: 13-978-0-692-12418-5.

About the Author

The Babe is the author's forty-year journey from spiritual infancy to realizing a balanced Christian walk toward spiritual maturity and enlightenment. Ms. Hawkins's unwavering commitment and service for the abandoned and abused of our society through adult-child protection has demonstrated her courage and devotion toward the suffering of God's kingdom. Ms. Hawkins is the proud recipient of the Kay Courtney Courage and Devotion Award with Tyndale Theological Seminary's bachelor of arts Bible and theology program.

www.ingramcontent.com/pod-product-compliance
Lightning Source LLC
Chambersburg PA
CBHW031327060726
47590CB00003B/1358